ENDORSEMENTS

Dennis Walker and his wife, Lynnie, are outstanding, mature ministers who have been used powerfully by God to faithfully bring the gospel to many nations and people.

This is a book of nuggets... precious revelations of truth that have come from a lifetime of seeking the Lord. The insights contained in this book will feed your spirit.

Patricia King
Founder of XPmedia.com
Phoenix, Arizona, USA

Be thrust forward into your calling and equipped to seize the Holy Spirit's direction. Dennis Walker's book, *Catching The Initiatives of Heaven*, gives us insight on how to do the works of Jesus in the way that He commanded us to do them. By activating your spiritual senses, you can see and hear from heaven and bring miracles to earth.

This book has the potential to transform your daily life and therefore, transform your world. I highly recommend this practical book for learning how to move in miracles.

Ché Ahn
President & Founder of Harvest International Ministry
Pasadena, California, USA

God didn't call just some of us to "do the stuff." You have all you need within you to hear the voice of God and know the will of heaven and set it in motion.

Dennis' book will show you how. Read it and receive your upgrade to move higher in the Spirit than ever before!

Lou Engle
Founder of "TheCall"
Kansas City, Missouri, USA

I have known Dennis Walker for years. He is a powerful man of God with an extremely powerful and anointed ministry, with signs following. His new book, *Catching The Initiatives of Heaven*, tells story after story of hearing God's voice, seeing vision and acting on them and watching as miracles happen! I believe this book will inspire you to no end. Dennis' passion is to let you know that you can do this. He encourages you to get started and tells you how! What a blessing this book will be to your life. Read it and see if you don't agree.

Mark Virkler
Author of "How to Hear God's Voice"
Buffalo, New York, USA

Catching
THE INITIATIVES
OF HEAVEN

Catching
THE INITIATIVES
OF HEAVEN

*The Key to Accessing the Power of Heaven
for Every Need on Earth*

DENNIS WALKER

Dunamis Publishing

Printed in the U.S.A.
ISBN: 978-1-4507-2994-9

You may contact Dennis Walker about speaking at your conference or church.

Contact Information: Dunamis Resources
2413 Jubilance Point Ct.
North Las Vegas, NV 89032, USA
1-702-461-0508
www.DunamisARC.org

Cover & Interior Design: Carina & Christian Oechsner
carinachristian@gmail.com
www.NewCreativeIdeas.com

Dunamis Publishing

Dunamis ARC—Apostolic Resource Center is like the leaven of the kingdom of God. "A little leaven leavens the whole lump." Our goal is to supply resources that lead people into the Holy Spirit's power *(Greek: dunamis)*, setting the stage for the last great revival.

To those who dare to live bi-dimensionally,
bringing the power of heaven to earth.

*Special thanks to Lynnie Walker, my wife,
to Tracie Ogando, our daughter,
to Becky Grimshaw,
and to Christian and Carina Oechsner.*

You made this project possible.

CONTENTS

FOREWORD

My life with Dennis has been an adventure! He has always been a trailblazer, going after the cutting edge both in the natural and in the spiritual. And I, Lynnie Walker, the lover of calm routine, have learned to go with the flow and enjoy the ride! Previously, for example, I was terrified of flying. Now I hop on a plane with Dennis almost every month, heading to yet another country to preach another message and to activate more people. I need to tell you a bit of our background so you can see where we are coming from.

Dennis and I, raised as pastors' kids, met as teenagers at a church conference in Texas. (He from California and me from Florida). Three years later in 1974 we were married in the high jungles of Peru, at the lower levels of the Andes Mountains. I had been raised most of my childhood in Peru by my parents who were missionary pastors. Dad performed our wedding. Folks brought flowers from the jungle and I made my wedding dress and cake. A year later, our first of three children was born. (They are all married now, serving the Lord and have given us four grandchildren.)

Dennis and I served the Lord in Peru for those six years with no support from the United States, so we lived at the level of the people we served—not something we recommend, but useful in getting to know the people and culture. Dennis planted crops and hunted and I washed clothes in the river. We had no electricity or running water. I played the accordion and taught school and Dennis played the guitar and preached—often traveling by land, by air and by river. This part of our lives is detailed in a book I wrote entitled

Heavenly Encounters.

We moved to Las Vegas, Nevada in 1985 where we became pastors of Spanish- and English-speaking churches. We were impacted by John Wimber's teachings, which launched us to a new level in healing. One of the first ladies we ministered to was healed of thirty-nine tumors!

In 1995, we were greatly impacted by the Toronto Outpouring. Our lives, our children—who had very real encounters with God—and our church would never be the same. We moved into greater levels of God's manifest presence and power in healings and miracles. Dennis was even used to raise two people from the dead in Las Vegas. One of those stories made the newspaper with the headline, *Miracle Baby.*

Lest you think it is about us, it's not. It's about a loving Father in heaven. It's about the power of Jesus' shed blood. It's about hearing from heaven and obeying. It's as easy for God to heal a headache as it is for Him to raise the dead. Any one of us can learn to catch the initiatives and instructions from the One who has all the power and do it on earth. And along the way, He is faithful to take us through breakings to keep us humble and to form us as His vessels of glory.

Dennis had a life-changing experience in 2002. After attending an Open Heavens conference in British Colombia, Canada, God told Dennis to buy a tent when he returned home and to spend time with Him inside the tent. God said He would meet him there. So when Dennis arrived home, he immediately bought a pup tent, set it up in our house and began spending extended times in the presence of the Lord. He began being caught up to heaven. Jesus showed him amazing sights in heaven. Jesus would preach sermons to him and then Dennis would preach them at church!

One day I commented to Dennis, "I like it when you spend time in the tent." "Why?" he asked. "Because you come out tender." The time in God's presence was changing his very character! At the same time, there was an increase of miracles. Dennis began to move into a new level of words of knowledge about people, sometimes revealing their names and illnesses. Dennis moved into a new level of revelation as well. Some of the simple, yet deep, truths in this book, came during those times in the tent. Some of the revelations will come in future books.

Around 2003, we turned our church pastorate over to others and were launched apostolically to oversee a network and also to travel the world in ministry.

In 2004 in Las Vegas, God led us to open a training center called Dunamis to activate people to hear and see from God and to activate them in the miraculous works of Jesus so they could take it to the streets. As people are touched by the power of God, they are led to know Jesus. I could tell you many miracle testimonies, but suffice it to say, if God can do it in Las Vegas, He can do it anywhere!

Around the world, we have seen people launched, not only into a life of miracles, but into areas of political influence, media influence and business influence as they were given ideas from heaven. Often these were unlocked prophetically over them.

I can think of one instance in Brazil when a man thought Dennis was just trying to be nice, by prophesying destiny in governmental influence over him. A year later he apologized to Dennis, telling him what he had thought. He told Dennis that he had indeed moved to a high position of influence with government leaders. This man had suddenly received an idea from heaven one day and everyone liked his idea. His next appointment was with the president of Brazil! I believe it had been unlocked by the prophetic word over him.

We believe God is raising a prophetic people who will learn to access heaven and catch the initiatives of heaven and bring heaven's wisdom and power to earth. Joseph and Daniel in the Bible rose to the highest positions of influence because they could hear God's voice. This will be true for everyone who is willing to learn to listen and see what is being done in heaven and bring it to earth.

Dennis has always said that the easiest way to know if you are hearing from God is through results. For example, you can measure results in the prophetic flow (you are either wrong or right) or in healing (either they are healed or not)! You will make mistakes as you learn, but that is how you will grow. The Bible says, "We know in part and we prophesy in part." It also requires us to discern, "Test all things; hold fast what is good."

So go try it at Walmart or at work, especially where you see someone with a need. Do it in a gentle, natural way. Watch yourself grow to greater levels of hearing God and catching the initiatives of heaven to bring answers to the world. Come join the prophetic army on earth.

I hope you will not only enjoy reading this book, but begin to try it!

Lynnie Walker

Author:
Heavenly Encounters
Ten Ways God Speaks

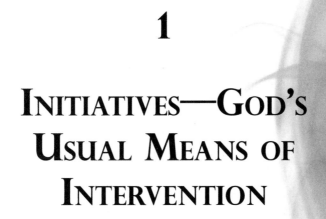

1

INITIATIVES—GOD'S USUAL MEANS OF INTERVENTION

I broke a toe one day and it became swollen, black and blue. My wife, Lynnie, came home and saw me in bed and looked at my foot. "You poor thing!" she exclaimed.

I answered, "I don't need pity, I need an initiative of heaven for my healing!" This was serious! I had to leave on a ministry trip in a couple of days and didn't want to be hobbling around. So Lynnie walked down the hall and told our friends, John and Glenna Miller, that we needed to hear from God for my healing.

They got quiet and quickly tuned into heaven—into Jesus. John said, "I just got a flash of a picture of something to do but it looks really silly."

"Oh, good, that's the kind that really works!" Lynnie exclaimed.

So they came down the hall to my room. John had received an "initiative of heaven" (a specific directive) for my healing. He saw a picture of Jesus pouring water on my toe. He grabbed a bottle of water, put a towel under my foot and poured a little water on my toe. "That's all I saw from Jesus to do," he said and left.

Within fifteen minutes all the pain was gone. I got up and walked to the couch in the living room. After another forty-five minutes, I looked at my toe and all the swelling was gone! Not only that, but all the black and blue was gone as well! Now, black and blue does not disappear that quickly in the natural. But my friend had accessed an initiative of heaven from the secret place through spiritual senses and the miracle occurred. I was totally healed and was able to walk around as though nothing had happened and make my scheduled ministry trip on time. This was not a formula to be repeated every time. It was specific for this case. It was an initiative from heaven.

Throughout the Bible, God's usual means of intervening miraculously in the affairs of men was through dialogue and instructions from heaven. God met needs and overcame problems throughout the history of the Bible—starting with Genesis all the way through Revelation—by speaking and giving instructions. When these instructions were carried out on earth, miracles happened.

Oftentimes people pray pointless, powerless prayers hoping that God will magically change that situation using somebody else and at some other time. But that is not the way God works. Throughout scripture people cried out and then got quiet and listened to God. He told them what to do and when they did it, things changed miraculously.

For example, in the Old Testament, the people cried out for water in the desert. God said take the rod and strike the rock. It was a particular rod, a certain rock, an instruction of action to perform and water would come forth. It was the divine initiative coming from heaven. As they obeyed, things happened. Miracles occurred.

You and I are going to do His works in His way. The only formula that I know of doing those works is to see and hear and obey. That is the way Jesus said He did it. In John 5:19 Jesus said, "The Son can do nothing of himself, but what He sees the Father do; whatever the Father does, the Son does just the same." The key to divine intervention for healing, deliverance or provision is to catch the initiative of heaven by hearing and seeing in the Spirit. Scripture says very clearly, "My sheep hear my voice." You can do this whenever you have someone come to you with a need for a miracle. Instead of praying a prayer and not really expecting God to speak or show you anything, expect Him to show you things! Expect Him to speak instructions to you; so make time for that. Pray the prayer, "Lord, we ask you to touch him right now and here is the need." Then you get quiet, "Lord, we wait on you right now; speak to us." God will bring spontaneous pictures, words and thoughts to convey His instructions for the need at hand.

Another biblical story is Naaman the leper. He came to the prophet of God from a distant land to receive healing. He traveled with a group spending all the time and money to get there and he came loaded with treasure expecting to pay for his healing. When he finally met with Elisha, the message he got was less than inspiring: "Dip seven times in the River Jordan and you will be healed." Water had never healed him before! Little did he know it was much more than water. It was the initiative of heaven that just happened to include water!

DOING JESUS' WORKS

In Matthew 10, Jesus commissioned the disciples to go and do what He had been doing—to preach the kingdom of heaven, to heal the sick, raise the dead, cleanse the lepers and cast out demons. That was how the kingdom was to be extended. They were not just to preach in word, but in deed; the two-edged sword of proclamation and demonstration.

Jesus later sent the Holy Spirit to His disciples, baptizing and empowering them to fulfill what He had called them to do, until "the uttermost parts of the earth" were reached. The first disciples began this work, but did not reach the uttermost parts of the earth during their lifetime. Therefore, the same empowerment for doing the works of Jesus is still in effect for us today. God wants to draw every people group on earth into His kingdom, opening the door for His return.

WHY MANY DO NOT ACCESS HEAVEN'S POWER

Many are missing out on extending this "help from heaven" because they believe the signs and wonders stopped with the first apostles. They don't expect God to heal or move in miracles today.

Others aren't fulfilling this mandate because they live in a futuristic idea of the kingdom. They believe that the power of God is left for some future event, not realizing that the kingdom of heaven is both now and future. We can have kingdom *dunamis* (Greek word for "mighty power") right now as we access heaven, understanding that the fullness of the kingdom is yet to come when Christ returns.

Others simply have not understood how they can access this help from heaven to extend to others. They don't understand that God has provided all we need to move in miracles today, including giving us spiritual senses to access His power.

Another reason people do not walk in the miraculous works of Jesus is that our present Christian culture has made us content with the accumulation of knowledge as an end in itself. Sadly, much of the present church system could continue without the work of the Holy Spirit. We have said,

"Bless our works," instead of saying, "Lead us by your Holy Spirit." But change is coming!

God is raising up an army of people who are saying, "May Your kingdom come and Your will be done, on earth as it is in heaven," and are willing to be a vessel for extending this help from heaven by doing on earth as He is doing in heaven.

DOING IT!

"Is there someone here who has a scar on their hand and the little finger doesn't work?" I asked. A lady standing by the back door raised her hand, so I called her forward.

It was the end of a conference meeting in Pucallpa, Peru and after teaching, I had decided to wait on the Lord to see what He would do. It was at that moment I saw a mental picture of the hand with the scar below the little finger and the non-working finger.

As the lady came forward, I continued to wait and see what exactly the Lord wanted to do. The Lord spoke a word of knowledge that she had been in a fight with someone she loved. I asked her, "Have you been in a fight with someone you love?" She began to weep and said, "I just had a fight with the man I live with. He threw me out of the house. I was wandering down the street, saw people standing in the doorway here, stuck my head in and you asked if there was someone here who had a scar on their hand with a finger that didn't work."

By then I knew the greatest need she had was to receive salvation. When I asked her if she would like to receive Jesus into her heart and life, she said, "Yes!" There was no need for much convincing after the Lord had revealed so much already. So I led her in a prayer to receive the Lord as her Savior.

Then I asked the Lord if there was anything else for her. He said to simply lay hands on her and bless her. So I asked permission from the lady, "May I lay hands on you and bless you?" She said, "Yes!" So I laid hands on her and began to bless her in the name of Jesus.

Suddenly she began to jump up and down and then began to speak in tongues for several minutes! When she was done, she looked at me and asked, "What was that?" I had her sit with one of the pastors to explain all that had just happened to her. The Lord never led us to pray for healing of the lady's finger, but simply used it to identify her.

The next night, the lady brought about twenty of her friends and family to the meeting. They all gave their hearts to the Lord!

By hearing and seeing things from the Lord (through the activation of the spiritual senses of sight and hearing), the Lord had impacted a lost soul and brought her into the kingdom. She was also filled with the Spirit to empower her in her Christian walk. The Lord used her to bring her family and friends to the Lord. Like the woman at the well, she said, "Come and meet someone who has told me all about my life!" Help from heaven had come to the city of Pucallpa, Peru.

2

FIVE STEPS TO WALKING IN THE INITIATIVES

There are five steps to walking in the initiatives and seeing miracles occur. Five is the number that represents grace. Grace is not only unmerited favor, but it is God's enabling power. Grace is His power working through us.

CRY OUT TO GOD

The first step is to cry out to God. Many do not receive from God because they do not ask Him. They run to their own resources. They run to the medicine cabinet, run to take out a loan or run away when there is a relational problem. But God wants us to ask Him first and see what He wants us to do about our problems.

When the children of Israel were being chased by the armies of Egypt, they all cried out to God, "Save us!" It really doesn't matter who cries out to God, as long as someone does!

GET QUIET AND LISTEN

After you cried out, then stop crying out in order to hear God. The next step is to get quiet and listen. Most Christians think prayer is only about talking, but they don't realize that it is like using a telephone. You talk and then you listen. God is waiting to give some answers from heaven. In fact, you can use the same ratio of listening to speaking as illustrated in how our bodies were created, with one mouth and two ears. Listen twice as much time as you spend speaking!

Focus on Jesus

The third step is to focus on Jesus. We can quiet our mouth, but we can't quiet our mind. So we must learn to focus our thoughts on Jesus. Colossians 3 says to set your mind on things above, where Christ is seated at the right hand of God.

Catch The Initiatives of Heaven

Fourth, is to catch the initiative for the need at hand by hearing what Jesus says or seeing what He is doing. Tap into the spontaneous flow of pictures and words to catch the heavenly initiatives. God wants to speak to you about what you have asked Him. And it usually comes with an instruction from Him that will bring the answer and solve the problem.

Obey The Initiative

The fifth and final step is to do what Jesus indicates. Make what you hoped for into substance, by bringing it from heaven into earth through your obedient action or words. You will become the evidence of the things not seen, as the power of the unseen kingdom is demonstrated in your life. Heb. 11:1 says, "Now faith is the substance of things hoped for, the evidence of things not seen." You will see the miracle become reality.

This is a pattern repeated throughout Scripture. Most of the time when God is answering prayers, He does it through instructions by His spoken word or through visions. The people in the wilderness were crying out for water. Moses prayed, "God, they are thirsty and they are going to kill me. What do we do?"

Moses didn't plead with God for water and then just

walk away. He didn't decide beforehand how God should respond, "Now God, we know you work in mysterious ways and we just believe for a million pots of water." He didn't try to make God fit into his preconceived theological framework through a series of wrong assumptions.

Many times we do this—we are assuming how God will act. This is demonstrated often when we pray, assuming God is going to use somebody else, somewhere else, some other time, some other way and not use us right here and right now. Our wrong assumptions rob us of the power of heaven. God wants us to catch an initiative right when we pray that will unlock the miracle.

Moses came to God, prayed and then caught the initiative of heaven. The initiative of heaven was, "Take the rod and walk over to that rock and strike it." The initiative of heaven overcame thirst on earth. 1 John 5:4 says, "Whatever is born of God overcomes the world." So he acted on the instruction and water flowed out.

Remember the Bible story of when the widow's sons were going to be sold into slavery. She cried out to God. She spoke to the prophet about her problem and then he cried out to God. Most of us would say a nice little one-size-fits-all generic prayer and think we have done our duty. Then we would say, "Now if God doesn't deliver them, then it is His problem and her problem." The truth of the matter is that we have not made the right assumptions. The right assumption is that God sends His Word. Scripture says He sent His Word and healed them. He sends His word to bring creative answers. He sends it to give "right now" instructions. God is pitching—do we have any catchers?

He is looking for available vessels on this earth to begin

to release the power of His creative word. Fortunately, He had a prophet who received the direction from God and came back to the woman saying, "Go and get vessels from all of your neighbors. Fill your house with pots and pans and jars and whatever vessels you can find—not a few. Fill your house." That was the first instruction. She went out and did that.

Then came the hard-to-understand instruction, "Now take that little jar of oil and fill the other ones." Now I am sure that she struggled with that one. "Wait a minute. There is only a pint of oil there and you want me to fill all those other vessels?" He said, "Do it." And she did it. Her obedience brought the miracle. The little jar continued to pour out oil until the whole house was full of oil. She sold it all and saved her family.

It is that kind of initiative that comes through divine directions from God to bring the answer to the needs. That is what God wants to do with each of us. Now, I believe He could do it without an initiative, just to show us He is sovereign. But I believe that most of the time God moves when we come to Him and He says, "You are my son. I am in relationship with you and I am going to tell you the thoughts of My heart concerning this. The thoughts that are initiated in My heart overcome every need on earth." As we walk in this dynamic flow of heavenly communication and powerful actions, then God's highest priorities are being fulfilled. The prodigal sons and daughters are being brought home and in the process we are learning to know our God!

When you start catching initiatives and start bringing them to earth, you will see everything around you change. The sick will be healed, the dead will be raised, the captives will be set free, provision will come and wisdom and knowledge will come. You are the ladder to heaven. You are the connection of heaven's power to earth through the Holy Spirit. Begin to catch the initiatives of heaven and watch heaven merge with earth!

EVERYONE CAN DO THIS!

A s followers of Jesus Christ, we have been authorized to take dominion here on earth while we are in our physical bodies. Not even the angels have such dominion here. They are simply commissioned to assist us as we are moved by the Holy Spirit. As we pray, speak or act, they move with us.

We are the connectors of heaven's power to earth, just as Jesus was (John 1:51). As we see into heaven and do on earth as He is doing in heaven, there is a release of miracles, signs and wonders. This is how Jesus moved with His Father here on earth, leaving us an example.

Jesus says that whoever believes in Him will do His works (John 14:12). That means this power is available for a particular kind of person: the one who believes in Him! It's not only for the "professionals". The Lord is wanting to change the mindset of His church so that leaders and members alike realize that every one of them can do the works of Jesus. They can heal the sick, raise the dead and they can bring people to Christ.

We must lose the mentality of the "anointed one" in the church doing everything. The purpose of the five-fold ministry—apostles, prophets, evangelists, pastors and teachers—is to equip and commission all believers to do these works (Ephesians 4:11, 12). We should all be "the anointed ones"!

"He who believes in me" also includes "she". The coming revival will not fully come until women have been empowered and restored to their place in Christ. The Bible says in 1 Corinthians 11:3 that man is the head of the woman. Because of misunderstandings of what this means, many women are stifled in ministry because of the concept that men are somehow better. But in that same scripture, it also says that the head of Christ is God and the head of man is Christ. How did they model headship? God said to Jesus, "Come up here and rule with Me." Jesus says to mankind, "Come up here and sit with me in my throne." So the message to women is, "Rise up and let us rule together—let us do the works of Jesus together." God is calling both men and women to do His works.

Men are also being called in a special way to do Jesus' works. Some churches have a majority of women, but God is raising up men to see their authority in Christ and to see the mighty potential they have to do the works of Jesus.

Youth and children are included in doing the works of Jesus. They will especially be used in the coming wave of the Holy Spirit. Joel 2 says that in the last days He will pour out His Spirit "on your sons and daughters".

Ephesians 2:10 says we are created for good works—and not just any good works. The works that were prepared beforehand. Jesus walked in these works so that we could follow Him. He came to earth from heaven to give us an example of how to walk. As He walked on earth (and on water), so should we!

As we become aware that we are called and empowered to do the works of Jesus, the question arises, *What are those works?* Jesus gives us a list of what those works are. He said in Matthew 10:7-8, "And as you go, preach, saying the kingdom of heaven is at hand. Heal the sick, cleanse the lepers, raise the dead, cast out demons. Freely you have received, freely give."

The first point in this passage is to preach. We are to preach the gospel of the kingdom of heaven, not just the gospel of salvation. Salvation is simply the entrance into the kingdom of heaven. Salvation is the way in—it's the door that leads to all the other aspects of the kingdom. If we focus on the kingdom of heaven we will see the power of the kingdom operate in our lives.

HELP FROM HEAVEN

I had an impacting vision years ago in which I saw a stadium filled with thousands of people who had come to see the many miracles, healings and resurrections that were occurring. I saw that secular businesses were there to sponsor this event and to broadcast it by television and other forms of media. I even noticed a particular brand of toothpaste that was one of the sponsors.

On the platform I saw a great banner that said *HELP FROM HEAVEN HAS COME TO EARTH.*

The Lord explained to me that He is re-contextualizing the message "The kingdom of heaven is at hand" into a language that the present generation can understand. The message of the kingdom should be shared this way, "There is help from heaven for you!" The original recipients of this good news of the kingdom of heaven were the Jewish people. They had carried the prophecies of the kingdom for many centuries. They knew that the kingdom would bring the help from heaven. But if you were to stand on any given street today and proclaim "The kingdom of heaven is at hand", people would think you were proclaiming the end of the world. That is not the message we are proclaiming. It is not a message of fear, but of astounding hope enveloped in the demonstration of God's power to help us in times of need. This comes as we learn to catch the initiatives of heaven. There really is help from heaven for you!

REACHING THE LOST

Catching the initiatives of heaven is about reaching the lost. The Lord wants us to quit trying to save the found and get out there and look for the people who are lost—those needing help. He wants to show Himself as the God of all. He is the Creator of all. He is the Redeemer. He wants to be evident to people and He will show Himself through the divine initiatives.

"Initiative of heaven" means "that which God starts" and what He starts He always finishes. Especially if He finds the right one to bring the breakthrough. When you see God's initiatives and start catching them and speaking them, they are not just your words, they are the words of the Creator spoken through you. As it says in 1 John 5:4, "Whatsoever is born of God overcomes the world." Whatever He initiates overcomes natural laws of health, finances, physics, medicine and any other natural law. John 15 says, "Without me you can do nothing." We move as a team.

We have the same testimony as Jesus had in John 5:19 who could do nothing of Himself apart from what He saw the Father do. He had absolute need of the Father and the work of the Holy Spirit to do the things that He did. You and I also have that same need. We can do nothing without Him. But with Him we can do all things.

PARADIGMS SHIFT—WORLDVIEWS CRUMBLE

Jesus wants us to be kingdom agents, engaged with people for the transmission of His power from heaven so that people would marvel. Marvel is what happens when worldviews fall. Worldviews are people's belief systems— what they believe is possible or not. We have seen people who say that they are agnostic, that they don't believe in God, but then we catch an initiative about them and all of a sudden they get goose bumps and are scared or in awe because it doesn't fit their worldview. It is a marvel. There is marvel manifesting all over them and old worldviews begin to crumble. Suddenly faith arises in their hearts.

John 5:20 talks about marveling. It says, "For the Father loves the Son and shows him all things that he himself does and he will show him greater works than these that you may marvel." I asked the Lord, "Why do you want people to marvel?" He said, "Marvel is the sound of world-views falling." God wants to show off His power through us. John 14:12 says, "The works that I do, you shall do and even greater works." The reason He wants us to do even greater works is so the world might marvel. People change their world-view or their belief system when they see a miracle. We saw it happen with the "woman at the Starbucks well". Coffee shops are a great place to move in this power.

We were invited for coffee at Starbucks by my brother-in-law, Jim Drown. He invited me and several of my family. We approached the counter to order our coffees and Jim popped up to the front and said to the guy at the cash register, "I am going to pay for the coffee of everybody in line." A lady had just walked in behind us and heard Jim say he was going to buy her coffee.

She protested saying, "No, no, I will buy my own coffee."

Jim answered, "I said I will buy for everybody in line and I will."

She agreed to let Jim buy her coffee. I don't think she understood she would now be in debt to listen to him.

Jim was probably thinking, "A cup of coffee for a soul. Not bad."

Jim and the lady waited for the order and the rest of us went to a table nearby. Jim introduced himself and made a bit of small talk. All of a sudden Jim said, "You have begun writing a book, but you stopped writing and God wants you to finish the book."

She was shocked. Her eyes got big (this is marvel) and she asked, "How do you know this?"

Jim responded, "God told me."

She said, "But I am an agnostic, I don't believe in God."

Jim looked at her and said, "That's all right, God believes in you and He wants you to finish your book."

She was still in shock when Jim added, "You have some partial deafness in your left ear and God wants to heal your ear."

The woman started trembling and said, "You are freaking me out!" (Again, this is marvel.) What she was not aware of is that her agnostic world-view was falling. Marvel is the sound of world-views falling.

Then Jim said to her, "I want you to pray with me right now and ask Jesus to come into your heart."

She replied, "I can't do that, I'm agnostic, I don't believe in God!"

Jim said, "You used to be agnostic, but now you have seen evidence that God is real and that He knows you and He is calling you."

She was trying to process this, when she exclaimed, "You are the third person who has spoken to me about Jesus this week!"

"Well, what does it take? Pray with me now." She ended up praying with Jim, then and there, to accept Christ as her Savior.

He brought her over to the table and said, "Here is a new sister in Christ!"

She still had a shocked look on her face and then asked me, "How do you hear from God?" Now this was a statement of faith, from a self-proclaimed agnostic. She no longer doubted that God existed, but asked how to hear His voice. So I started explaining to her, in just a few minutes, how God speaks to us. That when we are born again and receive the Spirit of Jesus in our hearts, that our spiritual senses are activated and we can begin to hear Him.

All of a sudden I said to her, "And God wants to heal your knees!"

She said, "You are freaking me out!" (The marvel continues.) "How do you know about my knees? Do you see something?"

I said, "No, there is nothing visible, but the Lord just said that you have pain in your knees and need healing."

She said that she used to do skydiving, had landed wrong and had wrecked her knees.

I asked, "Would you like to get rid of that pain?"

She said, "Yes, but don't put your hands on me, I'm still freaked out about all of this." (Hmmm, freaking marvel?)

I told her I didn't need to touch her. So I just spoke over her knees the words that I heard Jesus say.

She said, "My knees are getting hot."

I said, "Move them now."

She moved her knees and exclaimed, "The pain is gone!"

She said, "I think God wanted me to leave with tangible evidence that He is real, by healing my knees."

She then tried to leave but came back, still in shock, to see what more she could learn. Then our daughter, Tracie, said, "I see a vision of Spanish words, *Manos de Ayuda* which in English is *Helping Hands*."

She added, "I believe God will use you to help Hispanic women find jobs.

The lady responded in shock, "That is the name of my business. It is *Helping Hands* and I help Hispanic women find jobs."

This lady got hit so many ways and through several people. She had an encounter with a living God and it changed her life. That is what God wants to do wherever we go. His heart is for the lost. He wants to show Himself powerfully through us to the world.

We want to see revival and we want to see massive impact where people and nations are brought in. All we have to learn is how to walk catching the initiatives of heaven. I believe that the future revival is going to be all about people learning to walk under the initiatives of heaven, catching the things that God is doing and bringing those things to earth. They will be igniting the flames of revival wherever they walk.

ONLY A FEW ARE NEEDED TO USHER IN REVIVAL

Most people don't see healing or miracles happen partly because of pointless, powerless, pusillanimous prayers (small-spirited prayers), but also partly because they have a wrong assumption of how God works. They may believe God can and wants to heal, but that He is going to do it somewhere else or use somebody else. They think, "I am sure not the one qualified for this." My wife, Lynnie's, brother, Johnny Enlow, wrote an interesting book called, *Are You Weak, Small or Foolish Enough to Really be Used by God?* That is a great book because it shows that God is not only looking for the ones with the best image and every hair in place, nor the smartest or wisest. He is looking for the ones who are weak, small and foolish enough to be used by God. John Wimber used to say, "God will use those who are available."

God wants to use us all to give the message of His goodness to others. Once we have these things in motion, it's not going to be too much longer before revival breaks out. Think about the prophets in the Old Testament times. They were men who heard God, saw God and did His initiatives. Just one or two of them at a time was enough to stir up a whole nation.

What would happen in your city if there were a thousand, only a thousand, doing the initiatives of heaven out there on the streets? You would absolutely turn it upside down. What would happen if you only had a hundred of them? In Abraham's day, only ten people could have changed the destiny of Sodom and Gomorrah. After Jesus ascended, His twelve disciples turned the world upside down. We are learning to live our lives knowing that God is speaking to us, directing us and sending us.

Life is going to be different when we get to the point where we are aware that we are hearing and we are seeing. All we have to do is step out and test it. When you start doing that, then you are going to know that God really is showing up. He wants every one of us to be activated.

How many times a year do you pray for someone who asks for prayer? What is going to happen this year as you are called on to pray? Instead of praying pointless, powerless, prayers that are initiated from earth, stop and ask, "God, what do you want to do?" Just go with that flow. Expect that God is going to show you something. Expect that God is going to speak something and follow the flow of the Spirit. What is going to happen this year?

All it takes is one or two people around town saying, "Hey, go to that person and you will get healed, because I went there and God did this and spoke that. It changed my life." As more people step out to catch the initiatives of heaven, it will draw individuals and nations to His kingdom.

If you are dedicated to following the Lord this way, coming into a place of intimacy where you hear His voice and learn to follow Him, you could have a full-time ministry of miracles. Just speaking the initiatives of heaven over people and having that as a full-time job. One of the things that is motivating me is that I believe that the coming outpouring of the Spirit and revival is all about this. The sooner we catch it, the sooner we will see it poured out. God is waiting for us. He is waiting for us to get prepared. I believe that this whole concept of catching the initiatives of heaven and simply walking in them is what God is doing right now. He is preparing the church for His outpouring.

ROUGH CHARACTERS RECEIVE JESUS

Here's an example involving two of my brother-in-laws, Jim Drown and Johnny Enlow. Jim shared Jesus with a guy that was parasailing off the cliffs over the beach in Lima, Peru. Jim had talked to him two years before about Jesus and the guy basically cussed him out, so Jim left him alone. The next year he came back and the same guy saw him coming. Jim often will do something foolish or humorous to catch people's attention. So he walked up to the guy and said, "Hey, how about a free ride or half-off?" The guy was a really crusty guy and said, "You bring me two pounds of cocaine and a couple of whores and I'll give you a ride." Jim said, "I really came over here to talk to you about Jesus." When he said that, the guy said, "I'm sorry ... I'm sorry I said that stuff. I didn't know that you are a Father." Being from a Catholic country, he thought Jim was a priest. Jim started talking to him and for some reason the guy started listening to him.

Lynnie's brother, Johnny, was also there with Jim and they started praying over the guy. Suddenly Johnny felt by word of knowledge that there was something wrong with his ankle. The guy said it was true and agreed to receive prayer. They laid hands on his ankle and all of a sudden the guy got hit with a bolt of power from the Lord! He started running and jumping up and down. He had been in an accident on his hang-glider, crashing into a building and damaging his leg and he hadn't been able to walk very well since then.

He was instantly healed! He had a buddy, kind of an associate in his business and he started hollering at the guy. He said "Hey, God just (censored) healed me!" He was still cussing, yet both those guys accepted Jesus right there on the side of the cliff. They started bringing other guys who had businesses there to receive prayer. It was a little mini-revival on the side of the cliff and it was because there was an initiative of heaven. Somebody got healed and all of a sudden there was an invasion of the gospel into that area.

LOOK AND LISTEN FOR AN INSTRUCTION

G et out of your religious box, overcome the temptation of presuming to know what God is going to do. Stop speaking Christianese, using Christian terminology and traditional prayers. Don't pray generic prayers that are the one-size-fits-all prayers, basically the same prayers used to bless the food or heal the sick, just changing the names and wording a little. In fact Jesus never prayed for the sick, He simply spoke the words of His Father or performed actions based on what He saw the Father doing. Look and listen for the instructions from heaven.

Throughout the Word of God, most of the time when God was ministering and answering prayers, He did so through specific instructions. People cried out to God, He gave instructions, they did it and miracles happened.

Moses received the initiative to stretch out his rod over the Red Sea. The rod was just a plain, simple stick. Can you see this picture? A whole army coming with the sole purpose of destroying you and God says stretch out the stick! What? A stick against a whole army? Ahhh, but it was more than just a stick! It was the stick plus the initiative of heaven. Someone needed to receive the initiative and act upon it. God's initiatives are small, like a grain of mustard seed, in comparison to the great needs. Stretching out a stick was a tiny, foolish action in comparison to the great sea before them and the mighty army behind them. But it just took mustard-seed-size faith to act on it.

Moses obeyed, stretched out the rod and the miracle

happened. The waters parted and the Israelites went across on dry land even as the pillar of God's fire held the army of Egypt back.

You don't need "sea-parting faith" to part the sea, just as you don't need "cancer-healing-size faith" to heal cancer. You just need enough faith to hear and to do what God shows you, even if it is a small action. This simple obedience to the initiative becomes the greatest manifestation of faith. Your faith is demonstrated in the action that brings the miracle.

Lynnie and I have been doing this for a number of years. It started when we were trained in some of John Wimber's classes and with Bob and Penny Fulton. We were trained to stop, listen and then act. I came from an old Pentecostal model that was like this: when somebody needed prayer, you had to get psyched up and you had to get the anointing going. If you were really anointed then you were going to shout. You were going to shake the person. You might spit a little when you were shouting. That was our model for praying for people. We would have people come forward and we would grab them and shake them, shout for thirty seconds, command healing and then it was over. We did our part, but was anything happening? Usually not. The only healings we saw were what I call "accidental healings." Accidental healings are when you just accidentally happen to hit on what God wanted you to do anyway. You happened to hit on that initiative from heaven accidentally. But you don't have to wait for accidental healings. You can start sharpening your senses and waiting on God and letting Him give you the initiative from heaven that brings change to that situation.

WOMAN HEALED—MARRIAGE SAVED

L ynnie and I have seen literally hundreds—maybe even thousands—of people who have received healing or deliverance from all kinds of problems. I remember one of the first healings we saw for a man and his wife about to go through a divorce. She had gone to a doctor and they found a tumor on her cervix and she was about to go in for a biopsy. This couple had actually come for prayer for their marriage. The Lord gave us clear words of knowledge about what had happened in their lives to bring them to this point. We spoke to them about the root of their marital problems. They confirmed we were hearing correctly. We led them to give up the past offense and their marriage was put back together. The divorce was canceled and the wife called the next day asking, "What did you do to my husband? He is a different man." Later she went in for a biopsy and there was no tumor.

That was the first time we purposefully stepped out on the instructions of heaven for people and waiting on God to catch His initiatives. This has become even clearer and more defined for us since we really started spending time in the secret place with the Lord. We have received so many "downloads" from heaven about situations and circumstances. We are seeing a new cutting edge in ministry as we receive the initiatives of heaven and bring real answers to people's lives.

All of these things are accessed by faith. You must have expectation that God will use you and have expectation that you can catch an initiative from heaven. I want you to know that I believe that every one of us, at God's initiative, can walk on water. Do you believe that? That is not really a big deal. Peter walked on water. But he did so at Jesus' bidding.

I teach a lot on healing and I get people coming up to me saying, "Would you come and pray for this one or that one?" I am sad about that, because they still are not catching it. My goal is to activate everyone. It may be that God is speaking to them and they just need to be aware of it. Scripture clearly says they can hear: "My sheep hear my voice." Every need we face by the initiatives of heaven is an opportunity for our growth and development. When you catch this, you won't give your growth opportunities away. God's heart is to bring many sons into glory and you are those sons and daughters He is bringing into glory.

OBEDIENCE—NOT AS HARD AS WE THINK

All this is accessed by simple faith. God spoke to Abraham and said, "Leave your father's house." Do you know where faith started? When he took his first step. It was just simple obedience to the directive of God. And when he did so, he became the father of the faithful.

Faith is that simple for us today. It is not something that you have to struggle with. Jesus said that if you have faith as small as a mustard seed—a very, very small seed of faith—that you can move mountains. I didn't understand that for so long and I always had a different interpretation. I thought that you plant the seed and it grows and before you know it, you can move a whole mountain. But not even a mustard plant can move a whole mountain. I understand today that it is so simple, it is so small. It is about what He directs you to do and you simply obey. It is the simple step of obedience to His instructions.

Some of the acts of obedient faith that Jesus performed looked strange. I think He did this on purpose so that we would really get an understanding to obey whatever the Lord tells us to do. How many of us would spit and make mud and put it in somebody's eyes? The two things you never want in your eyes—somebody else's spit and dirt! Jesus put them both in a man's eyes, told him to wash and he was healed. He did it to teach us something. He never healed a blind person the same way twice. This was just one of many blind people that Jesus healed. I picture the Lord in heaven saying, "We have got to find a different way to do this so that they don't fall into a rut and think it's a formula."

It is not a formula. It is hearing and seeing and obeying. I think the Father said, "You spit and make mud and stick it in his eyes." Jesus caught it, did it and the man was healed. The Father is probably laughing as I'm telling this. It is written there so that you and I will know it is not about formulas, it is not about you reciting certain scriptures, it is not about you coming to some understanding as to what causes blindness. If we follow this model of hearing and obeying each time, the blind will be healed. But more importantly, God's will is accomplished.

If you try to repeat what you did before to move in healings or miracles, it might accidentally work on one or two people. But that is not really what God wants. He doesn't want you walking around doing accidental healings; He wants you to heal the sick, raise the dead and cast out demons. The way you do that is by catching the initiatives of heaven. It is through relationship with Him. What you see, you do. What you hear, you say.

Exercise Strengthens Skills

I don't hear perfectly—none of us do—and I don't see perfectly. But this one thing I know, the more I use the initiatives, the more it will grow. The more I spend time with the Lord in intimate relationship, the more it will grow. So there are things that I can do that will cause these abilities to grow and there are things I can do which will cause them to shrivel up and die. What you must do is avoid all the things that cause your senses to darken and become hindered in any way and then do all the things that enhance your ability to receive from God. One of the things that you can do that enhances your ability to see and hear is to step out and do the little things that He is telling you to do right now.

Obeying Even When it Sounds Strange

My wife and I were living in Mount Charleston, Nevada, in a cabin which we were borrowing while we were having a house built down the mountain in Las Vegas. We would often invite guests to come and visit us. We were having one of those times of fellowship when some of my family came up there—my sister, Dara and her husband, Craig. Craig was complaining about problems he suffered with diabetes and pain in his legs. He said, "I don't have good circulation in my legs."

In the middle of talking about his legs, all of a sudden I saw something that I believed was an initiative from heaven, but it looked weird. But finally I thought, "Well I am just going to go for this." So I looked at Craig and said, "Craig, I just saw something. Can I do it on you and the worst that could happen is that it could mess up your hair. Can I do it?" He said, "Yeah, go for it." What I had seen myself doing was taking a small throw blanket off the couch and throwing it over his head and then whipping it off. There is no place in scripture where it says, "Thus saith the Lord, thou shalt whip blankets off of people's heads to see them healed." It doesn't say that, but it could be that the Holy Spirit was testing me to see if I would do what He was showing me to do.

Well, I grabbed the blanket and threw it over his head and left it there for just a split second, then whipped it off his head. There were a couple of ladies behind us talking, one of them with her back to us and she got hit with the wave of power that came off of him. I felt the power go by me, blasted the lady and she went flying against the wall and screamed, "What was that?" Meanwhile, my sister, Dara, on the other side got hit with a blast of heat from the Lord and she started crying. I asked her, "Why are you crying?" She said, "I felt it." Craig was there in shock.

I went on to talk to somebody else, I came back and Craig was standing in front of the fireplace lifting his feet up and down on the hard surface. He was there for a long time and said, "You know I couldn't stand on a hard surface like this for very long without having strong pain and right now I have absolutely no pain in my legs." There again, we saw evidence of things happening. There were waves of power and as a result, pain was gone from somebody's legs after whipping a blanket off of their head.

Now if you try that again, about all you will get is messed up hair and maybe even a sour look on someone's face, because it's not about blankets and whipping them off of their heads, unless God tells you to do that. But this illustrates the fact that you can begin to see into heaven and catch pictures and catch directives that God is speaking to you and then begin to move on those things. Those are the initiatives of heaven. And God loves for us to move this way, because it is based on relationship with Him.

About a week later, we had a couple (pastors of one of our Spanish churches in town) come to spend the day with us. They came to receive some impartation. So we spent the day going over scriptures and ministering over them. At the end of the day when they were about ready to leave, my wife, Lynnie, said to me, "You know she has been diagnosed with a cyst on one of her ovaries. She is in constant pain and they want to do a hysterectomy on her. They told her that she has to do this right away because it is dangerous. Can we pray for her?" I said, "Yeah, let's do it!"

What we do in situations like this is to just get quiet. We say, "Lord, what are you doing? We are here and we are available." We don't ask, "Do you want to do it?" because we know He always does. It is more about, "How are you doing it? What do you want to do?" So I was there waiting and listening and all of a sudden I saw a picture. But I didn't know what to do with this picture I was seeing because it was rather strange.

I am learning that you even go with the strange instructions. Jesus said to pray this prayer, "Your kingdom come, your will be done on earth as it is in heaven." I think this is more literal than we have understood. He is calling us to do on earth what we are seeing in heaven. Just like Jesus did. So I was standing there praying and asking the Lord, waiting on Him to speak or show me something and I finally got a picture. I thought, "Well, I am supposed to reproduce this on earth."

The picture I saw was the Lord with His head up against this lady's abdomen right where her ovaries would be, like He was listening. But I thought, I am not comfortable putting my head there, so I asked Lynnie if she would put her head there. So Lynnie knelt down and put her ear right against the lady's abdomen like she was listening. I said, "Okay, Lord, what is next?" Sometimes there will be other instructions that He will tell you to do. He said, "Put your hand on her head." So Lynnie was there with her ear up against her stomach area and I put my hand on her head and immediately a prophetic word came. The word was, "The Lord says He hears your faintest cry." That is all I said.

When I said those words, she began to violently shake. I have never seen her jerk, shake or fall. She is a "Rock of Gibraltar" sort of person. But she was violently shaking and finally she fell as her husband caught her. He gently lowered her to the floor. She was shaking, crying and laughing, all at the same time on the floor. This went on for a while and finally I asked what was going on. She said, "I have never felt anything like this before." I said, "Help her stand up," so they helped her stand up. She was standing there, still laughing and crying and then began moving her leg up and down. I was thinking, This is strange. I asked, "Why are you moving your leg like that?" She said, "All the pain left and it feels empty."

She was moving all around trying to feel the pain and couldn't find it. She said the pain was gone and it felt empty. I asked her a couple of weeks later, "Is there anything there?" "Nothing is there." A month or two later, "Is anything there?" "Nothing is there. It is gone!"

What a wonderful thing to see that God loved the woman we had prayed for on the mountain so much, that there was a specific message she received: "God loves me and He hears my faintest cry," and then He took the cyst out.

There again, it was an initiative from heaven that looked strange. I didn't know quite what to do with it at first, but all I did was reproduce on earth what I saw in heaven. I am becoming aware and having more and more faith that so much of what I am seeing in my mind are spontaneous pictures from heaven of what I am to copy on earth.

I get simple pictures and they're not ecstatic visions with angels or rays of light from heaven; no nice music or thundering voice. I see pictures like any other mental picture, but I'm seeing it right when I'm waiting for God to show me something. And when I see a picture, I'm learning to go with it. If it's just me, usually what I do isn't going to hurt anyone anyway. And I say usually, because there was one time that God had me do something that I struggled with.

I was in a meeting waiting on the Lord and He said, "There are some men here with prostate problems; call them forward." So I gave the word of knowledge and called them forward. Two men responded.

I was standing there waiting on the Lord in front of

the first guy asking, "God, what do you want to do to bring healing to this man?" The Lord said, "Hit him real hard in the stomach." I started asking, "Now are you sure about this? This guy may have an enlarged prostate and maybe it's delicate. If I slug him in the stomach I could burst it. I don't know what all could happen, Lord." And the Lord said, "Do you want to see healing?" And I said, "Yes." He said, "Hit him real hard in the stomach." I still asked the Lord, "Are you sure? God, is this you?" The Lord said, "Hit him real hard in the stomach." Finally, I started negotiating. I asked, "Can I hit him with my hand open?" And the Lord said, "Yes, hit him with your hand open, but hit him real hard."

The poor guy was there with his eyes closed. Hindsight is always pretty good. In the future, I would probably warn him and say, "Listen, tighten up because I am going to hit you," or at least ask his permission. But I didn't. I let him have it! I pulled my arm back and—wham! I knocked the air out of him. He was there kind of gasping. Finally, he just toughed it out and accepted it.

The second guy saw the whole thing. The look on his face was something else! He was looking back at his wife as if he was saying, "Mommy, what do I do?" But then all of a sudden I saw some resolve come. He probably decided, "Okay, if he can take it, I can take it." So he started tightening up with his eyes shut. I pulled my hand back to let him have it and the Lord said, "I didn't tell you to hit him." I dropped my hand and just stood there. I asked, "Lord, what do you want me to do here?" He said, "Place one finger on his forehead, then declare healing." So I laid a finger on him and declared healing. I think the first guy may have felt cheated or abused or something, because he was now watching what I was gently doing with the second guy! The good news is that both of those men came back the next day and said every symptom was gone. In fact, the man whom I had hit really hard invited us to a banquet at his house to celebrate his healing!

Be careful about a strange initiative. Be really sure. Dialogue with the Lord. Ask Him, "Come on, are you sure?" He will talk to you and He will give you direction. Then get permission from the person.

Usually what I do isn't risky, so I just go with it. Then if it seems I missed the direction, I can say, "Oops, I missed it. Sorry, let's try it again." There is no condemnation if you make a mistake, but the results are worth the possible embarrassment.

I believe that when we are born again, we become partakers of the heavenly kingdom and we become those who are tasting the good things of the age to come, now. Jesus said that if we follow Him, if we deny ourselves and leave all other things behind, we will have much more now in this age and in the age to come. We can have foretastes of the kingdom of heaven now, while we await the fullness of the kingdom to come. We can live a life of miracles today, as we catch the initiatives of heaven.

CANCER HEALED AFTER GOD REVEALS SECRETS

A man in Peru was brought in on a stretcher. Doctors had recently operated on him for stomach cancer. They had opened him up and found the cancer was too widespread. They closed him back up, told his family to take him home as he was going to die within the week. That was the week my brother-in-law, Jim and I did our outdoor crusade in Pucallpa, Peru. The sick man's daughter came to me saying, "Can you pray for my father?" I told her, "You go back and stand by him and I am going to ask God what He wants to do right now." She went and stood by her father. All I did was say, "Lord, they have a need. What are You going to do about this?"

I got quiet there in the middle of all the worship, 110 decibel speakers—huge stacks—blaring loudly. (Yes, you can get quiet and hear from God in the midst of that.) So I was listening and the Lord gave me two words of knowledge about this man's past; things that he had been involved in and where this cancer came in. I didn't know whether God was going to heal him. He didn't tell me that for sure. All He did was give me two pieces of information that were initiatives from heaven and now I had something to act on.

I walked over to him, knelt down and I spoke into his ear, partly because the sound system was so loud and partly because it was private information. I asked him if he had a daughter he had disowned. He said, "Yes." I then asked him if he had been involved in witchcraft. He nodded his head, yes. I asked him if he wanted to repent of both of those things and give them to God and he nodded his head, yes. I led him in prayer as he gave it up to God and then I asked, "God, what now?" He said, "Tell the cancer to go." That is what He told me, so I looked at the man, I stood up, then I spoke, not to the man, but to the cancer and said, "I command you to go in Jesus' name!" While standing there, the Lord said, "It is done." I have learned that those words mean I am done, so I walked away. I turned my back, not having seen one change in his body, but the Lord said it was done. So I walked away.

The next night, the man came back walking to the meeting! He climbed up the steps to the platform with a little help. Remember he had just had surgery. It was amazing. He climbed up the steps, came to the microphone and said, "I accepted Jesus last night. This man over here prayed for me and when he turned his back and walked away, the pain left!"

I have learned that even though you see nothing and the Lord says, "It's done," the fact that you turn your back and walk away is a step of faith. So I had turned my back and walked away. The man went home and ate for the first time in thirty days. He had been hooked up to an IV, but suddenly was able to eat again. He had no pain.

He was an older man and all of his kids and his grand kids came to the Lord after his healing. The whole family joined a church we oversee there. About a month later we were back in that city and the man's family was still there, he was still there, everybody was fine and he still had no cancer. A year later I checked with their pastor again by telephone and the man was still healed and the family was serving the Lord. God healed this man when the doctors had opened him up and said, "Nothing we can do. He will be dead in a week." The healing came by an initiative from heaven.

Woman's Foot Healed by Simple Command

I visited Atlanta to minister some time ago and we were praying over a group of people. There was one lady who looked like she was having a hard time by the look on her face. I wasn't sure if she wasn't believing what we were saying or possibly she was in pain. She hesitated, but then came forward, so we prayed for her and prophesied some things over her. Almost immediately the Lord spoke something—it was an initiative from heaven. I looked at her and said, "There is something wrong with your feet. Do you have a need in your feet?" She nodded her head. I had someone else come over and lay hands on her feet and I began to pray. I said, "Lord, right now restore the bones of these feet in Jesus' name. I just release that on you." I didn't do much more than that. I've learned that when Jesus released initiatives from heaven, they weren't verbose, they weren't wordy, they weren't that eloquent, they weren't preachy, they weren't exhorting, they weren't even prayers. Most of the time they were short and simple commands.

Jesus said things like, "Stretch out your hand." Something enormous happened because the man simply stretched out his hand. Most of us, if we had gotten a directive like that, would have added another couple of paragraphs about stretching out your hand. Jesus didn't see the need to add to what the Father was giving. He simply repeated what the Father said and did what the Father showed Him to do.

So back to the story, I spoke over the lady's feet. I looked at her a little while later, she had her shoes off and she was doing toe stands. I asked, "What is going on?" She exclaimed,

"Look at my feet!" I looked at her feet and said, "Well they look normal to me." She said, "That's the point!" She said that many years earlier she had been riding a horse and the horse had fallen and rolled over on her leg and foot and crushed her foot. She said that there was no bone in her foot that was intact. Every bone had been broken into small pieces. Doctors had performed surgeries to put it back together but it never had come together right and her foot was in constant pain. As a result, her foot had been turned out to the side a bit, in a frozen position. Now it was completely straight and all the pain was gone!

3

THE TENT—A NEW BEGINNING

A ll of this exploded into my life through a series of encounters I began having with God starting in 2002. I had attended a conference on "The Open Heavens" with Todd Bentley, Patricia King, Jill Austin, among others. I was the Senior Pastor of Harvest Rock Church in Las Vegas, Nevada at the time. I had traveled with four others from our church (including my daughter, Kelly) to attend the conference in Abbotsford, British Columbia, Canada. My best friend, Jim Drown, had introduced me to Todd earlier that year and we had decided to meet up at the conference.

We spent a glorious four days receiving teaching on our access to heaven as well as receiving impartation through the laying on of hands. I could feel the presence of the Lord moving powerfully in the meetings. But the real outpouring started the day we left the conference to return home.

We had flown into Seattle and rented a car for the short trip across the border into Canada. When it was time to return, the five of us piled into the car and immediately became overwhelmed with the presence of the Lord that filled the car. It was like gathering burning coals together and seeing the fire blaze up. My secretary, Maria, began to shake violently in the back seat. I was thankful that my friend, Robert, was driving—I think he had more experience driving under the influence of the Holy Spirit!

We had left Canada knowing we would have six free hours before needing to arrive at the airport, so what we should do with this time was on my mind. As we were driving along I suddenly saw a vision that we were in a beautiful park spending our free six hours with the Lord. I shared this vision with everyone in the car only to discover that all five of us had just had similar visions. My daughter, Kelly, had just seen a vision of a lake, Maria had just seen a vision of a forest and the rest of us had seen a vision of a park. While contemplating the significance of these visions, we came to an exit sign on the freeway indicating that the next exit was for *Lake Forest Park*! I pointed to the sign and shouted, "That's our exit!"

We pulled off the freeway at that exit and when we got to the cross-street the Lord spoke to everyone in the car, "Turn left." We turned left and had a forty-five minute adventure where the Lord spoke to all five of us concerning every turn. We came to a "T" intersection where we saw a park right on a lake directly across the intersection. Was this it? "No," the Lord spoke. "Turn left." We continued following this road around the lake until we came to a heavily forested area and the Lord said, "Slow down and look on the left." We slowed down and began looking on the left and came quickly to a small sign that simply said *Park Entrance*.

We pulled into this park and came to a parking lot where we parked the car. When Maria got out of the car her eyes landed on a scene she had seen two weeks earlier in our listening prayer time at church. She had seen a gently descending green field with white daisies sprinkled throughout. In the vision she had run to the middle of the field and laid out in the presence of the Lord. She had shared this vision with those of us present. This was the scene that now greeted us. She began shouting, "It's my field, it's my field!" She ran out to the middle of the field and laid out in God's presence.

I continued on into the park and came to a large table-shaped stone under some pine trees. I climbed up on the stone and laid myself on it. I began to tell Jesus, "Here I am a living sacrifice to you." I began to feel waves of the presence of God sweep through me.

I am not totally sure how long I stayed there, but after a while the Lord spoke into my thoughts very clearly. "When you go home, buy a tent. I will meet with you in the tent. I will restore to you the Feast of Tabernacles." I knew that the Feast of Tabernacles was part of the last feasts of the year for the people of God. I knew that the Feast of Passover had been fulfilled on the day that Jesus died on the cross; the Feast of Pentecost was fulfilled on the Day of Pentecost in Acts 2; and that the Feast of Tabernacles was to be fulfilled as part of end-times events.

I got very excited and jumped off the stone table to go find somebody to tell what I had just heard. I found Robert and Joann talking together close by and started excitedly telling them what I had heard.

While I was telling these things, my eyes fell on a peculiar sight. There was a tree stump right behind Robert and Joann that was about twelve to fifteen feet high. The top had been cut off as well as all the branches of a twenty-inch diameter pine tree. When my eyes landed on this tree I heard Jesus ask me, "Can this tree live?"

"Why, Lord?" I asked.

His answer astonished me. "If I were to judge My church right now and cut off all the branches that have not produced My fruit in My way, this is what My church would look like."

Suddenly I screamed to the tree, "I command you to live!"

Time passed very quickly after that. We made it to the airport and finally to Las Vegas around 10:00 p.m.. But before driving home from the airport I stopped at an all night store—Las Vegas has many—and bought a tent.

I arrived home after 11:00 p.m. and immediately started pushing furniture around in my living room and setting up a tent. My wife came out of the bedroom to discover I had arrived and saw I was putting up a tent in her living room.

"Doesn't that go outside?" she asked.

"No, this one goes inside and with me in it," I countered.

I then proceeded to tell her all about my encounters with God that day. I asked her to protect my time in the tent, "Handle the phone calls and if they knock at the front door, tell them I have gone to heaven." This was the first day of a new beginning for my life!

HEAVENLY ENCOUNTERS

I began spending time in the tent. I would go into the tent, put on headphones to eliminate any outside distractions and listen to instrumental music. I began to close my eyes in the natural and open my eyes in the Spirit. Very quickly I began to see things in heaven, seeing various scenes in heavenly places. I knew that my body was still in the tent, but I was seeing new things as my eyes were being opened. What I was seeing was very detailed and very clear. Also I could feel the presence of Lord on me as I would have these times of encounter.

One of the first visions I had was of a field in heaven where I was walking with Jesus. This field had a pathway marked through the center of it. I was following Jesus, noticing round stones that were marking the path. As I looked at one of the stones, I noticed the stones had eyes and were looking at me! Stones with eyes! How can that be?

Then the Lord answered me and told me that everything is alive in heaven—everything is made up of living material.

As this thought began to soak into my mind, the Lord asked if I remembered the tree in the park that had all the branches and the top cut off. I remembered it well.

Then He said, "When my church begins to spend time with me in heavenly places, that which was dead will come alive." He then asked me, "Do you remember the rod of Aaron that budded?"

I remembered that they placed the rod of Aaron in the Holiest place overnight and in one night a dead stick had come alive. It produced new branches, new flowers and full-grown fruit in one night.

The Lord said, "This is what I'm about to do in my church today. I'm about to bring my church into heaven and have it permeated with life. That which has been dead will spring forth with new life. A nation will be born in a day."

The Lord showed me many things in heavenly places and I began to spend more and more time in the tent. I heard His voice, I could feel His presence and I saw things. My spiritual senses began coming alive as I waited on God in the tent. Many times the Lord would teach me things—showing me scriptures. I would begin to type and write notes about the things that God was telling me. Most of what I teach today came out of those moments in the tent. Even to this day new things continue to come as I spend time with Him in heaven.

Three Levels of Evidence

I have become aware that there are three levels of evidence that confirm the reality of our experiences with God. That we don't just test these experiences based on how we feel or by the warm fuzzies that may occur. He wants us to look for the true evidence that shows that these are heavenly realities. As I have continued to spend time in His presence, I have become aware of three levels of evidence.

The first level of evidence is character change. I became aware of this when one day, as I came out of my tent, my wife commented, "I love it when you spend time in the tent."

"Why is that?" I asked.

She said, "When you come out of the tent you come out tender."

Tender is not my normal state! But as I would spend time in His presence, it would have a tenderizing affect on my life. His presence on my heart and life was producing character change.

The second level of evidence is the increase of the power of God in our lives. There would be an increase of power for healings, for signs and wonders, for prophecy and for words of knowledge. Very accurate prophecies and initiatives began to mark my life. With this new ability to hear and see, I could catch the initiatives of heaven more clearly. I saw a greater level of activation into the works of Jesus.

The third level of evidence is when we have common experiences with other people in heavenly places. If the things that I'm seeing and experiencing are my own invention, then others will not be able to see them. But if these are heavenly realities, then it's possible that I could have an encounter with someone else in heaven who could tell me exactly where I was and what I was doing. I have had these kind of experiences with others who saw what I was doing and then later told me. This confirmed to me by solid evidence that it was not just a fantasy but it was a heavenly reality.

DIVINE FRIENDSHIP

Jesus is all about you learning to hear Him and relate to Him and get intimate with Him. To catch His heart, hearing the beatings of His heart. Learning to hear the instructions that He gives to you.

Out of an overflow of a love-relationship with the Lord, you will learn to catch initiatives from heaven. You will catch an initiative to heal someone, to do the works of Jesus or to receive information about someone you witness to on the streets. Maybe you will also start catching an initiative about your own spiritual condition—where your heart is. You'll start hearing from God about how you are relating with your husband or wife. You'll start catching initiatives about how to raise your children. You'll start catching initiatives about how your job is going and about your finances. You'll start catching initiatives in all these areas because it is all about relationship with the One who cares about every part of your life.

There is nothing about your life that God doesn't want to be involved in. He wants to be involved in every aspect of your life and He wants you to be so plugged into Him that you are living out of the resources and life of heaven. That is what Jesus did and He wants you to have life more abundantly.

SENSES ACTIVATED IN THE SECRET PLACE

I expect any or all of the spiritual senses to function when I spend time in the secret place with God. Matthew 6 says to go into your room, shut the door and pray to your Father who is in the secret place. He is waiting for us. When we come to Him, all sorts of amazing things can happen. We get plugged into Him who is the very source of life as we come into His secret place. Spiritual senses come alive and then they grow as we use them.

So the fruit of spending time with Jesus in the secret place is: (1) Sharper senses to more accurately catch the initiative of heaven. (2) A greater level of productivity in the fruit of the kingdom of heaven (more salvations, more healings, more provision and more miracles of wisdom). (3) Increasing hunger for the things of God. (Doing the works of heaven increases your hunger for heaven.) (4) A drying up of the appetites of the flesh ("Walk in the Spirit and you will not fulfill the lusts of the flesh" Gal. 5:16).

All of these benefits are produced when we allow the Holy Spirit to redefine prayer. So much of our prayer has been the initiatives of earth, our words to God in heaven. It is saturated with our works and our sweat, when in reality that is not what God is looking for. I can see a picture of

God in heaven saying, "Chill out! Let's just spend some time together." We need a fundamental change of perspective. It is all about fellowship with God. Our time of prayer is not so that we can spout off and then leave, but so that we can exercise the spiritual senses, seeing, hearing, feeling, smelling and tasting what it is like to be close to God.

COMMUNION WITH GOD AS THE SOURCE OF PROVISION

In Matthew 6, right after the portion of verses on communion with God, it talks about provision. Did you know that every need can be met in the secret place? As our senses are activated to hear or see things in the Spirit, He will show us what to do about our finances. We can access provision from the secret place.

One night we were attending a meeting in someone else's church in town. During offering time, Lynnie and I prayed and felt the Lord told us to give an offering of $600. Our budget was very tight and this was not "extra money" that we had! But we had learned that as we give in obedience, it unlocks God's blessings. I went to put the check in the offering, a bit shocked at the amount the Lord had told us to give. On my way back to my seat, two people walked up to me and stuffed checks into my shirt pocket. (Understand: I was not the guest speaker, nor was I a leader in that church.) When I checked later, there was a total of $5,050! I don't think this would have come my way if we had not given in obedience to the Lord. This is birthed out of times of intimacy in the secret place, learning to know His voice. Giving that is birthed from directives from heaven produces provision that "doesn't make sense." It is kingdom finance.

Years ago, we owned a private business but were struggling financially. We went to prayer, asking God for more work because we needed more money. We were already working long hours and raising up a Spanish church as well. We were burning the candle at both ends, but needing more provision. I'm glad that God knew what we were needing even if we worded it wrong.

I got quiet to listen to God's answer. He said, "Get a paper and pen." I got the paper and pen.

He said, "Write down these four names as I give them to you."

"Ready, Lord," I responded.

He had me write down four names of commercial real estate management companies that were supplying us with ongoing work. "Okay, now what?" I asked.

He said, "Now I want you to call these companies and tell them you can no longer work for them."

"Lord! I am asking for more work not less!"

"Just do it," He responded.

I have to admit my heart sank. He had told me to cancel working for four of my regular clients. I was shocked! I wanted more income, not less and this did not make sense. But I had learned to obey God's voice. So I called and told those four clients that I could no longer work for them. Amazingly, from that point on, we worked less hours and made more money and we stopped struggling financially. We ended up having a lot more time to dedicate to raising up a church. I learned that as we take time in the secret place, the Lord gives us directions for our finances.

FINDING HEAVEN'S INITIATIVES IN THE SECRET PLACE

In the secret place, we can tap into healing, whether it's physical or emotional. His very presence can heal us or He can give us an instruction—an initiative from heaven—that will bring healing.

One day our daughter called us by phone saying she was having terrible pain in her body. We prayed a simple prayer, but nothing seemed to change. We continued holding her before the Lord asking for an initiative. A couple of days later we were driving on our way to a meeting when I "got it." I received an initiative. A specific instruction for her healing. I called our daughter and asked her to set the cell phone on speaker phone and then to lay it on the part of her body that had pain. I then spoke to the body and commanded the pain and inflammation to go. This is what I had seen from heaven to do.

We arrived at the meeting and entered the worship service. Suddenly we received a text message from our daughter. All inflammation and pain was gone and she was totally healed! By the initiative of heaven.

The Holy Spirit can show us how to relate with our spouse, how to raise our children and other details of our personal lives in the secret place. One time when my wife and I were having a disagreement, I went to God in "complaining prayer." I got still to hear what God had to say about it. He told me to go tell Lynnie.... "Yes, I'll go tell her!"......but God said to tell her she was right! What? Yet I obeyed and told her God told me to tell her she was right. That simple act of obedience changed our relationship. Lynnie began going to God about issues, knowing I heard from Him and that He would speak to me. So God can flow toward us with miracles of wisdom from the secret place for personal direction and blessing.

In the secret place, He can give us His burden for prayer, sometimes concerning people we don't know. One night my wife, Lynnie, was told to pray for protection for the people in Wisconsin. She did not know anyone there, but she obeyed. She crawled into our prayer tent and wrote "Wisconsin" on a piece of paper and prayed for their protection. A couple of days later, the news reported that tornados had blown through the state of Wisconsin, destroying many buildings, stores and churches, but that not one person died. In the secret place, God tells us what to say in prayer, (an initiative from heaven), we say it back to Him and miracles happen! Isn't that amazing? It's so simple, yet so profound. It is prophetic prayer. We hear and we say. We see and we do.

I believe we are going to see a church that knows how to live and walk and interface in the Spirit more than any other generation through living in the secret place and through activation of the spiritual senses. The Bible says the glory of the latter house is going to be greater than the former house. The Lord is not coming back for a weak church, but He is coming back for a glorious bride without spot or wrinkle and mighty in the manifestations of God. She will reflect His glory to the world as she spends time looking at Him in the secret place.

INTIMACY WITH GOD RELEASES POWER

The only way to truly connect with heaven and to develop the spiritual senses, is to have a personal relationship with the Lord in a quiet place and to know Him above all else. Our life-flow comes from Him. Moving in miracles must be based on knowing Him.

Matthew 7: 21-23 says, "Not everyone who says to Me, 'Lord, Lord,' shall enter the kingdom of heaven, but he who does the will of My Father in heaven. Many will say to Me in that day, 'Lord, Lord, have we not prophesied in Your name, cast out demons in Your name and done many wonders in Your name?' And then I will declare to them, 'I never knew you; depart from Me you who practice lawlessness!'"

All of our activity and service to the Lord must flow from a relationship of knowing Him. Otherwise, it is religious activity and not a love relationship.

Dunamis power is released from this place of intimacy. It takes us from worry to faith, from restlessness to rest, from carnal thoughts to spiritual perceptions. The natural mind is at enmity with the Spirit and so must be quieted. (1 Cor. 2:14; Rom. 8:5,14; Ecc. 5:1-3). We must be emptied of ourselves to be filled with Him. We must focus on Him.

There is a need to set aside time and a place for the Lord. Yes, we should be open to the Spirit throughout the day, but we also must set aside personal time to quiet ourselves before Him. We must learn to tune into spontaneous thoughts and pictures and words that He gives, as His way of speaking to us. He is concerned with every area of your life and wants to live with you and through you. All He is waiting for is for you to begin to focus your thoughts on Him.

INCREASE YOUR CONNECTION

Y ou can increase your connection to Jesus and the Father by being baptized in the Holy Spirit. He quickens your spiritual senses to a new level. The Holy Spirit within you connects your spiritual senses to heaven. Information can flow back and forth. The Word of God is understood at a deeper level when you are baptized in the Holy Spirit. The Bible comes alive with new meaning. The Holy Spirit is the one who leads you into all truth. (Jn. 16:13). As you are baptized in the Holy Spirit, you have power to become greater witnesses to those who don't know Jesus. (Acts 1:8). Words of knowledge, healings and miracles increase when you are baptized in the Holy Spirit.

Jesus connected with heaven after He was baptized in water and the Holy Spirit came on Him and remained upon Him. Right after this experience, He said in John 1:51, "Most assuredly, I say to you, hereafter you shall see heaven open and the angels of God ascending and descending upon the Son of Man." He lived in a flow with His Father in heaven by the Holy Spirit. You also will flow more freely with heaven as you are filled with the Holy Spirit. The ladder of connection is formed from earth to heaven through you!

Another way to increase your connection to the flow of God's power is by hanging around others who move in the Holy Spirit. Their giftedness seems to overflow to those around them. Prophets impart the prophetic. Those who move in healing carry a mantle of healing that extends to those around them. Whatever anointing you hang around, will grow on you!

Your connection to the flow of God's power will also increase as you step out into what God has given you. If you listen to the Lord throughout the day and do what He says to do or say, then it will grow. Whether it's at work, at your job, at school or at the store, He wants you to increase your connection to Him. Putting a demand on the power of God through your sensitivity to the initiatives of heaven actually increases that flow. Removing blockages, such as fear or distractions, increases inflow and being active in doing the works of heaven increases outflow. Both have a great impact on the fluid dynamics of the River of Life as it flows through you.

Learn to give out what you have so flow will increase. Learn to give it out in a natural way. For example, "God wants me to tell you He loves you." Or "Do you have a sister who is sick?" If they say "no" then just say, "I'm sorry. I'm learning how to hear from God and I must have missed it." If they say "yes," you can ask God what to say next, such as, "I sense that God is healing her right now." God wants to train your senses in the secret place with Him, so you can take His power to the world.

4

SPIRITUAL SENSES

I often ask people how many senses they have and they tell me five (or sometimes that they have that "sixth sense"). Actually, they have ten senses if they are born again. Five natural and five spiritual. That is why Jesus could explain, "Though seeing, they do not see; though hearing, they do not hear or understand." (Matt. 13:13). They heard and saw in the natural, but not spiritually.

According to the writer of the book of Hebrews, spiritual maturity is defined by having spiritual senses exercised in the discernment of good and evil. "But solid food belongs to those who are of full age, that is, those who by reason of use have their senses exercised to discern both good and evil" (Hebrews 5:14).

Spiritual senses are regenerated when we receive our new birth in Christ. In John 3:3 Jesus told Nicodemus that unless a man is born again he cannot see the kingdom of heaven. If you put that into positive words, it means that once you are made alive in your spirit (born again), you can see the kingdom of heaven. Spiritual senses are activated. We are recreated in the Spirit through our new birth and what was dead now becomes alive.

In fact, when you are born again through faith in Jesus Christ, you become a complete human being. You now have your full set of *ten* senses instead of just the five you were born with. You have the five natural senses along with the five spiritual senses. Just as the natural senses give us interface with the natural world, so our spiritual senses give us interface with the spiritual world. The spiritual senses are the mirror image of the natural. The ten senses allow you to interact with both dimensions, natural and spiritual.

Jesus told Nicodemus in John 3:5 that unless a man is

born of water and the Spirit, he could not enter the kingdom of heaven. Born of water means natural human birth and born of the Spirit means spiritual birth. Both are important to walk in God's plan for our lives here on earth.

1 Corinthians 2:14 says that the natural man does not receive the things of the Spirit of God, for they are foolishness to him, neither can he know them, for they are spiritually discerned. Therefore, the only way we can access the things of the Spirit of God is through the activation of our spiritual senses by the Spirit of God.

Spiritual senses are needed to bring help from heaven to earth, to extend God's kingdom rule on earth. It is through the activation and use of the spiritual senses that we relate with our heavenly Father, receive initiatives born in heaven and bring heaven to earth. It is how we create the "ladder connection" to heaven.

ACTIVATING THE SPIRITUAL SENSES

Matthew 25:1-13 says, "The kingdom of heaven is like ten virgins who took their lamps and went out to meet the bridegroom…While the bridegroom was delayed, they all slumbered and slept. And at midnight a cry was heard: 'Behold, the bridegroom is coming; go out to meet him!'… Therefore watch, for you don't know the day or the hour when the Son of Man is coming."

We could say that the five foolish virgins were the ones with only five natural senses and the five wise virgins were the ones with all ten senses activated, including the five spiritual senses. The latter were the ones who both heard and watched with their spiritual senses. They kept their lamps filled with oil of the Holy Spirit's flow inside of them. They didn't deactivate their senses through slumber.

God is calling His church today to have the spiritual senses awakened to see, hear, smell, touch and taste in the Spirit. If the last days revival will be a prophetic revival, such as Joel 2 describes, then it is important to learn how to move in the spiritual senses.

We live in a season where God is sharpening our ability to live in the Spirit and know in the Spirit. Spiritual senses are sharpened through being filled with the Holy Spirit. He wants you to be baptized in the Holy Spirit and then be in-filled again and again, as happened with the disciples throughout the book of Acts.

Scripture tells us that we see in part, we know in part, we prophesy in part. That is true. We will still all make mistakes. We will see things wrong. There will be times when God wants to do something that we just don't catch. The thing that I know is that we can sharpen our abilities. We can sharpen our senses and we can begin to expect God to speak.

Spiritual senses grow as we saturate or "soak" in His presence. As we spend extended times listening to Him, our senses are sharpened and we are saturated by His presence. What God wants you to do is learn to simply get quiet to catch His initiatives. His initiatives come in so many different ways. They come through spontaneous flow in your seeing and in your hearing, your feeling and in your sensing in the Spirit, as you focus on Him and yield to the Holy Spirit.

Spiritual Maturity

We live in a culture where accumulation of knowledge becomes an end goal in itself. One feels mature if they know a lot. They go from conference to conference to accumulate more knowledge. But the Bible is clear that there must come practice, activity and exercise of what one knows. This defines maturity. This is meat. Jesus said, "My meat is to do the will of Him who sent me" (John 4:34). To put it another way, the milk of the Word is information only, while the meat of the Word is doing what you catch from heaven to do on earth.

Maturity also suggests responsibility and partnership in the works of the Father. When asked how He did the works, Jesus referred to the use of spiritual senses in doing what He saw the Father doing (John 5:19). Jesus shows us that having sharpened senses to relate to the Father is not an end in itself. It is also for the purpose of carrying out kingdom objectives on earth while we are here. This is the responsibility aspect of our relationship with Jesus.

The Five Spiritual Senses

Spiritual Sight

Spiritual sight is one of the five spiritual senses. It is the ability to see pictures from the Lord. These are often called visions. They are pictures in the imaging area of the mind, which are inspired by God. The screen is not evil, only the movie you project there can be evil. Some Christians shut the internal screen down because they are afraid of "vain imaginations". But God can fill that screen with His pictures as we yield it to Him. He created that mental screen to reveal His thoughts and images.

Visions come in different ways. Some people have quick pictures in the mind. They come in a flash. Others see clear visions in the mind and others have open visions or outer visions where they see things as clearly as natural sight. This can also be called a trance.

TRANCES, THE REAL THING

You may ask, "Isn't 'trance' a new age or occult term?" Actually, trance is mentioned in the Bible. The enemy only copies the real and that's where the word "counterfeit" comes into play. Visions, tongues and all the manifestations and gifts of God have been counterfeited by the enemy. Because of that, many Christians do not move into all that God has, nor allow it, because they are afraid of deception and afraid of counterfeit manifestations. But all they need is spiritual discernment to know what is real and what is false, which we will talk about later. They are missing out on so many of the blessings of God for their lives based on fear.

Let's think about a hundred dollar bill. A counterfeit hundred dollar bill can be reproduced, but in spite of that, we don't stop using the real bills. A counterfeit bill does not negate the value of a real hundred dollar bill. Think of what it can buy. And think of what we can access through activating spiritual senses, such as sight or vision.

In Acts 11:5 it mentions trance and vision at the same time: "I was in the city of Joppa praying; and in a trance I saw a vision, an object descending like a great sheet, let down from heaven by four corners; and it came to me." God took him into a trance and vision to speak clearly to him.

"While Peter thought about the vision, the Spirit said to him, 'Behold, three men are seeking you'" (Acts 10:19).

As a result of the open vision or trance, he was willing to go with these men to preach the gospel to the Gentiles for the first time, at Cornelius' home. Before then, the gospel had only been preached to the Jews. God needed to make a sufficient impact on Peter's mind to convince him of this new directive to preach to other people groups. Therefore He showed him a clear open vision in the form of a trance three times!

We know of people today who are having open visions. A lady pastor friend of ours in Peru was baptized in the Holy Spirit. She spoke in tongues and couldn't speak her own language for fifteen days! She had experiences of being caught up to heaven in the Spirit and when she came back, she started seeing written signs on people's chests. She would walk up to people and tell the secrets of their lives. Many were born again on the streets after she spoke the secrets of their lives and ministered to their needs. Often sins were revealed and people would come to repentance.

Let me explain about visions or revelations that bring correction and repentance. The prophetic ministry within the church should bring comfort, edification and exhortation. The scripture in 1 Corinthians 14 refers to what happens in a public meeting. In church gatherings, you don't usually have corrective prophecy going on. But there is still the ministry of the prophet that can be very corrective, that can confront sin and it is usually a position earned and respected in order to bring healing to God's people. I think that was what God was doing with our pastor lady friend in Peru.

A young visiting pastor came into one of the meetings where that lady pastor was attending in Peru. She looked over at him and saw a sign on his chest that read *Adultery*. She went to him privately with her husband and said, "You are in adultery, aren't you?" He got mad and said, "How could you say such a thing?" He denied everything. She said, "Well, I see it written on your chest. So I will ask God who you've been with." So she went home and prayed and the Lord gave her the woman's name and it happened to be somebody she knew. They went and confronted her and she broke down and confessed it all. Then they went and confronted the pastor and he confessed. They were able to get rid of sin in the church where the enemy was trying to destroy it. This gift brings healing, restoration and cleansing.

So there are outer visions where people see open visions with their natural eyes. There are inner visions or pictures in the mind. There are dreams, trances, angelic visitations and visitations by the Lord Himself.

I have had the Lord appear to me a couple of times in visions, while I was half-awake and half-asleep and preach whole sermons to me. On Sunday mornings I preached those messages! Through spiritual sight, we can see what He is doing or see what He is showing us.

Seeing Others as God Sees Them

Another kind of spiritual eyesight is the ability to see others with eyes of faith. God wants to open our eyes to His way of seeing things. To see the position we have in Christ; the potential we have in Him; and the power that is released as we follow His directions.

1 Samuel 16:7 says, "But the LORD said to Samuel, 'Do not look at his appearance or at the height of his stature, because I have refused him. For the LORD does not see as man sees; for man looks at the outward appearance, but the LORD looks at the heart.'"

With natural sight, we can look at someone who may look fine on the outward, but through spiritual sight God can reveal a deep need in that person's life. The Holy Spirit connects us to heaven to bring knowledge and an answer to their need. He then gives us a glimpse of their potential in Christ. Through spiritual sight, we can look past their needs and see their destiny.

Barnabas was able to look past Saul the Pharisee who had murdered Christians, to see Paul the Apostle of the Lord. Barnabas was used by God to open doors of ministry for Paul, when everyone else was afraid to associate with him after his conversion. Others only saw Saul the persecutor of Christians, but by the Spirit, Barnabas saw God's call on his life. He saw past "Saul the murderer" to see "Paul the man of God." Maybe that's why Barnabas' name means "son of encouragement." He encouraged Paul into his calling.

God is looking for a people with "Barnabas vision" who see past the defects in others and see the potential of God in their lives. He is looking for a people who will call people's destiny forth through encouragement.

Paul became a great apostle of the Lord. The Word says he was caught up into heaven and saw and heard secret things from God. He had a revelation of his position in Christ, not through his human religious zeal that he had as a Pharisee, but through the power of the Spirit released in his ministry.

SPIRITUAL HEARING

S piritual hearing is another spiritual sense. It is the ability to hear information or instruction from the Lord with spiritual ears. "My sheep hear my voice and I know them and they follow me" (John 10:27).

The Bible says in Mark 4:23, "If anyone has ears to hear, let him hear." He wants to awaken our spiritual senses to know issues of the kingdom. To know things from God. And to know things for people.

Spiritual hearing can come in several ways. It can come as an inspired thought. It can come through God's audible voice. It can come through an inner audible voice, where the message comes loud and clear inside of you. It can come through someone else's voice and bear witness in your spirit. As you get quiet and focus on the Lord, you can enter into a spontaneous flow of thoughts that help you hear from Him.

The messages you hear can come from one of three sources. It can come from your own thoughts. It can come from the enemy. Or it can come from the Lord. (This also applies to dreams and every other type of message that comes to your mind). The way you can tell the source of what you hear is through the fruit of the Spirit, both immediate and long term.

Galatians 5:22 talks to us about the fruit of the Spirit. For a moment, stop thinking of fruit growing on a tree and think of the verse this way: What the Spirit produces is love, joy, peace, faith and self-control, etc. If someone gives you a message they believe is from God, it should produce these good qualities and in this way we can distinguish the source. Even if it is a difficult word, if it produces good fruit, then it probably is of God.

One morning my wife, Lynnie, was writing in her prayer journal, conversing with God. Suddenly, she received a quick, inspired thought. "Someone in your family will be in a car accident today." The message came with peace, so she knew it was from God. She also knew that a seemingly negative word did not necessarily mean that she needed to accept it at face value. Often, the Lord gives information so we can actually pray against it or pray for protection or pray a reversal. So she prayed for protection for each one and that the blood of Jesus would cover each one.

Later that evening, our daughter Tracie arrived home late from the university. A friend drove her home. "Mom, you won't believe what happened. I was in a car accident that totaled my car," she said with embarrassment. "Well, how are you doing? Did you get hurt?" Lynnie asked. "No, it's the strangest thing. I don't have a scratch on my body!" Tracie exclaimed. God had protected her from harm in the accident. (Later, Lynnie thought that maybe she should have prayed protection over the vehicles as well!) God used an inspired thought to direct her prayer that morning, which brought a miracle of protection to our daughter.

The spiritual sense of hearing is a gateway sense. Adam and Eve lost spiritual sight in the garden of Eden, but retained spiritual hearing. When they sinned, they obviously had a change of eyesight. Scripture says that they had some new eyes opened when they ate of the Tree of the Knowledge of Good and Evil and what they didn't see before they now saw (shame, guilt, blame and natural wisdom). And what they saw before they now couldn't see. Previously, they saw God and walked and talked with Him in the garden. But after they sinned, they didn't see God walking in the garden. They only heard Him. So even after their fall into sin they could still hear God's voice. This is important. God left hearing open as a gateway.

The apostle Paul speaks about winning the lost through the foolishness of preaching. Preaching is so important for the lost because it comes through the gateway sense of hearing in the spirit. Even the unbelieving, unregenerate can hear the voice of God (though there is room for improvement).

Lazarus heard the voice of Jesus even though he was dead in the tomb. I believe this applies to people who are dead and lost in sin, yet can still hear the voice of the Lord calling them. That is why preaching the gospel is so important. As you speak the word of God, you are speaking life into their spirit. They can catch it and they will come to know the Lord. Then all the rest of their spiritual senses can become quickened and sharpened.

We are not supposed to be able to hear just a little, we are supposed to hear a lot. We are supposed to be able to hear God's slightest whispers. We are supposed to be able to be broken by the whispers of the Lord. We are supposed to be shaped and moved by His whisperings. The scripture in

Isaiah 30:21 says, "Your ears shall hear a word behind you, saying, 'This is the way, walk in it.'"

We have the example of Elijah who ran into the cave as he witnessed the wind, the fire and the earthquake, yet God wasn't in any of those. But the still, small voice of the Lord came and spoke to him.

God wants to lead us by His still, small voice. It is not necessarily accompanied by booming earthquakes, wind and fire. Those can be demonstrations of God's power, but I always look for the ongoing still, small voice of the Lord that brings understanding, correction and direction in my life.

I believe that when you are hearing in the spirit, you are hearing in the heart. How many times did Jesus say, "He that hath an ear let him hear"? Have you ever thought of that? Doesn't everybody have an ear? Well, yes, but what He is calling us to is spiritual hearing. I believe He is prophetically calling forth spiritual ears. Calling us to hear in the Spirit. The human mind, will and emotions are designed by God for communication with Him. We are given by God the ability to hear in the Spirit. His sheep hear His voice. (John 10:27) Our whole relationship with God is built on hearing Him!

One time I asked the Lord why He used the audible voice to speak to some people and why I have never heard it. He spoke to me that He usually reserves His audible voice for people who are spiritually deaf. If you look at the example of Paul the apostle, when he had his "road to Damascus experience" he was not a spiritual giant. He was spiritually deaf and persecuting the church, but then heard the audible voice of the Lord. It was because God wanted to really catch him and pull him in. He was apprehended at that point. He was arrested by the Lord.

I believe the same thing happened with Moses. Moses wasn't actually seeking God. In fact he might have been running from God until the burning bush caught his attention. God spoke to him audibly, as so excellently depicted in the movie, *The Ten Commandments*, starring Charlton Heston. But what was Moses' answer? "Not me! Can't you find somebody else?" I think this illustrates that Moses was no spiritual giant when God called him. He became a spiritual giant as he learned to recognize the still, small voice that would guide him his entire life. God calls out at times just to awaken people and draw them in. God is sovereign and He can speak to anybody audibly at anytime He wants, but I think most of the time God wants to speak to us on the inside. He wants to have His still, small voice speak to our hearts.

I asked the Lord, "Why is it that the way I hear your voice is so much like I hear my own thoughts?" He told me, "I created man with abilities to think and perceive, to see and hear on the inside as a means of communication." God's heart is to communicate with all of us all the time. How would it be if we all had to hear the audible voice. We would be saying, "Who me? Her?" It could get really noisy. It would be a noisy world, because God wants to communicate with all of us at the same time.

Psalm 81 says, "Oh, that my people would listen to me, That Israel would walk in my ways!" God longs for us to hear Him! We were created in His image for relationship with Him. Isaiah 32:3 says, "The eyes of those who see will not be dim and the ears of those who hear will listen." The Holy Spirit was sent to reveal God's voice to us (John 16:13).

Once you have learned to hear, you need to keep listening! Did you know you can lose your ability to hear? Hebrews 5:11 says, "You have become dull of hearing." Just as through lack of exercise you lose muscle strength, so with lack of use, you lose hearing in the Spirit. We must tune our spiritual ears to the voice of God and not to other distractions.

There are ways you can grow in your ability to hear or in your measure of hearing. Mark 4:24 says, "Then He said to them, 'Take heed what you hear. With the same measure you use, it will be measured to you; and to you who hear, more will be given.'" We used to apply this to giving financially, which could apply, when actually it is speaking of hearing. "...To you who hear, more will be given."

The Lord trains us to hear as we yield to Him. Isaiah 50:4 says, "He wakens me morning by morning; He wakens the ear to hear as the learned." Verse five says, "The Lord Jehovah has opened my ear and I was not rebellious, nor turned away backwards." We must quiet our own thoughts and receive His.

Spiritual Taste and Smell

One day I asked the Lord what the spiritual sense of smell is. Spiritual seeing and hearing were obvious, but what about the sense of smell? The Lord Jesus began to speak to my heart saying, "When I created mankind I placed your nose above your mouth for a purpose. I didn't create you with a blow hole on the top of your head like a porpoise. I placed your nose above your mouth so that everything going into your mouth must pass by discernment first. Your spiritual sense of smell is spiritual discernment."

Spiritual taste and smell are our ability to discern good from evil. Heb 5:14 says, "But solid food belongs to those who are of full age, that is, those who by reason of use have their senses exercised to discern both good and evil." Discernment is what keeps us on track. It keeps us from deception. Our spiritual nose knows!

Taste works with smell, because you smell food on its way to your mouth. The smell of the food helps create appetite and even initiates the process of releasing the digestive fluids. In the Spirit, we discern that something is good and we taste its goodness. We become "hungry" for the things of God. Psalm 34:8 says, "Taste and see that the LORD is good; blessed is the man who trusts in Him." Psalms 119:103 says, "How sweet are your words to my taste! More than honey to my mouth!"

When Jesus rebuked Peter, it was because of his lack of discernment in the Spirit. Peter was walking in man's emotion and thoughts, which agreed with Satan. That's why Jesus had to rebuke Peter as though Satan had spoken. Matthew 16:23 says, "But he turned and said to Peter, 'Go, Satan! You are an offense to me, for you do not savor the things that are of God, but those that are of men.'" He was not tasting or discerning the plan of God, but of man's natural wisdom. It did not seem to be a good idea for Jesus to die on the cross in the natural, but in the Spirit it was the means for salvation to come to the whole world. Later, when Peter was filled with the Holy Spirit he would understand this and would preach the first message of salvation that led three thousand to the Lord.

As we spend time with the Lord, we begin to pick up

His fragrance and spread it wherever we go. 2 Corinthians 2:14 says, "Now thanks be to God, who always causes us to triumph in Christ and He revealing through us the odor of the knowledge of Him in every place."

Eph. 5:2 says, "And walk in love, as Christ also has loved us and has given Himself for us as an offering and a sacrifice to God for a sweet smelling savor." Jesus' sacrifice smelled sweet to God.

In the Old Testament, in Exodus and Leviticus, it talks about sacrifices that were a sweet smelling fragrance to God. Those were natural burnt offerings. In the New Testament, Jesus became the perfect sacrifice to pay for all sin and now we no longer burn meat. Just as Jesus offered His body as a sacrifice on the cross, so we can offer our bodies as a living sacrifice as it says in Rom 12:1. The fragrance of a surrendered life can smell good not only to others, but to God Himself.

The Sweet Smelling Sacrifices

We can do things that smell good to God. Fragrances can either attract or repel people. Attitudes and actions all carry a spiritual aroma. In the book of Leviticus it says the sacrifices that were given were a sweet smelling savor unto the Lord. We also can make sacrifices that have a sweet smelling aroma.

One sacrifice we can offer, is the sacrifice of love. As we love God, absorb His love and extend it to others, it becomes a sweet smelling sacrifice to the Lord. We are called to be conduits of the fragrance of His love to the world.

We offer the sacrifice of obedience as we obey God's

direction for our lives. His inspired Word or heavenly initiative can give direction for a present situation. As we do His will on earth, it becomes a sweet fragrance to the Lord as we sacrifice our will for His.

The sacrifice of repentance is the evidence of a broken and contrite heart and is a fragrance that attracts the presence of the Lord. Psalm 51: 17 says, "The sacrifices of God are a broken spirit, A broken and a contrite heart—These, O God, You will not despise." As we embrace the breakings of the Lord, He promotes us to greater blessings in Him.

The woman who anointed Jesus' feet with ointment (Luke 7:38), filling the room with its fragrance, also anointed His feet with her tears in contrite brokenness and repentance before the Lord. This was the sweet fragrance that touched His heart and Jesus said, "Your sins are forgiven."

As we offer the sacrifice of communing prayer before the Lord, it rises as incense to the presence of the Lord. Revelation 5:8 says, "...having, each one, a harp and bowls of gold full of incense,—which are the prayers of the saints;" The Lord longs for us to have communion with Him. As we give Him our *cronos* (chronological) time, He give us His *kairos* (seasons of refreshing) time. When we give Him our day-by-day time, He shows up with His breakthrough time of visitation. In Acts 10 it shows that Cornelius' prayers had gone up before the Lord. The Lord responded by showing up in power by the Holy Spirit to this Gentile household.

Another sacrifice we can offer to the Lord is the sacrifice of praise. Hebrews 13:15 says, "Therefore by Him let us continually offer the sacrifice of praise to God, that is, the fruit of our lips, giving thanks to His name." As we praise Him, power is released to win mighty victories.

As we sacrifice our service to the Lord, it also becomes a pleasing sacrifice before Him. In Acts 6 and 8, Stephen and Phillip were faithful as deacons, serving to distribute food to widows, etc. The power of the Lord came upon them and they moved in signs and wonders even as they were faithfully serving in natural ways. God always rewards faithful service. Actually I don't know of any other way to become the living sacrifice commanded in Romans 12:1-2, than by living a life of serving Him by doing His will (initiatives of heaven).

The Lord crowns us with glory as we serve Him, yet we cast those crowns before Him, as it says in Revelation 4:10, giving Him all the glory. We are not saved by good works, but unto good works which He has prepared for us. (Ephesians 2:10).

The sacrifice of a generous heart rises as sweet incense before the Lord. In Philippians 4:18 it says, "But I have all and abound. I have been filled, having received from Epaphroditus the things which you sent, an odor of a sweet smell, a sacrifice acceptable and well-pleasing to God."

In Acts 10, it says that Cornelius' prayers and offerings ascended as a memorial before God and He responded by bringing salvation to his household. The Lord's blessings are attracted to giving. As one sows into heaven and sows into spreading the kingdom, blessings follow them and overtake them.

All of these sacrifices smell good to God and they attract His manifest presence. Just as God is attracted to pleasant fragrance, so should we by continually seeking the fragrance of heaven. When people dwell in the garbage dump, they can become accustomed to foul odors and don't even notice it.

We ministered to some very poor people in Mexico who lived in the dump and survived by digging through garbage, finding food to eat. When we went there to minister, we had to put mentholatum in our nose to be able to stand the smell. But they were so accustomed to it since they lived there every day. They were no longer aware of the stench.

We need to be so aware of the fragrance of heaven that when we are not in it, we miss it and long to come back to it. We can become used to the filth and smell around us and need to make a habit of taking a spiritual bath from time to time. Often when I shower in the natural, I also ask the Lord to cleanse me in the spirit from any filth I might have been exposed to from the environment I live in here in Las Vegas. This is so that I can carry the fragrance of heaven with me wherever I go and it can attract people to Christ.

When you are aware of the fragrance of heaven you will never be satisfied with less. Your spiritual sense of smell will discern when something is not right. You will become keen discerners of the truth.

DISCERNING GOOD AND EVIL

Your spiritual sense of smell is an important part of your ability to discern good and evil (remember Hebrews 5:14). There are three main keys to discerning between good and evil, right and wrong or truth and error. One way to discern what is right is by measuring it against the Word of God. Nothing contrary to the Word of God should be tolerated. For example, if you are told to lie, cheat or do anything forbidden by Scripture, then you can throw it out since it is against the Word of God which teaches honesty, love, forgiveness and holiness.

The next key to discerning what is truth, is that nothing added to the Word of God can be mandatory. If you are told to do something that is not clear in the Word of God, then you are under no obligation to receive it or do it. For example, if someone tells you that God told them that you must dye your hair blue, then you can ignore it since it is not a commandment of the Word. Those decisions are for you to make. Do you like blue hair? Scripture says nothing about hair color so it should neither be commanded nor forbidden.

The next safeguard and key for discernment is through the witness of others. 1 Corinthians 14:29 says when one prophesies, others who are present can judge. 2 Corinthians 13:1 says, "By the mouth of two or three witnesses every word shall be established." You can check prophetic words with others you respect. The final witness is what you sense in your own heart, especially when someone has given you a personal prophetic word. If you are getting ready to make a huge change in your life, you can run it by others you respect to see how they feel. But in the end you are responsible to make the right choice.

If we begin to train people in the body of Christ to use their spiritual sense of smell, it will absolutely open the door to a new level of maturity in receiving the manifestation of the Holy Spirit. Everyone will be able to test and prove what is happening and will only receive what is good. Learn to smell what you are about to eat! If it doesn't smell good… don't eat it!

We need to learn to apply 1 Thessalonians 5: 19-22.

Basically, Paul is telling us to allow the Spirit to show up, stop forbidding to prophesy, learn to test it and keep the good part. We must always remember that right now we know in part and we prophesy in part (1 Corinthians 13). In our training center, Dunamis, in Las Vegas, Nevada, we tell people that receiving personal prophecy is like eating fish—you don't take a big mouthful and swallow everything. You will need bone extractions afterwards. But you test each bite, remove the bones and swallow the good fish. You must learn how to spit! I think that is a good sign of spiritual maturity; knowing how to spit out the bad and eat the good.

FOUR THINGS TO TEST

There are four things that must be tested, according to scripture. First of all, every spirit should be tested, as it says in 1 John 4:1, "Beloved, do not believe every spirit, but test the spirits, whether they are of God; because many false prophets have gone out into the world." You must test the source (spirit). We must discern if a message is coming from the Lord or not.

We must also test every message. This means you are testing the content of the message. This includes messages taught, preached, prophesied, sung or written. 1 Corinthians 14:29 says that if someone prophesies, the rest should judge or discern it. Accountability is essential. In the Old Testament they stoned a false prophet. In the New Testament we can simply "stone" the false word or message. Is the content of the message leading on the straight path or is it polluted, diluted or convoluted in some way?

Every messenger must also be tested. You must test

the medium of communication. What do you do with evil messengers who bring a true message. This actually happened to the apostle Paul while ministering in Philippi, as recorded in Acts 16:16-18. A slave girl with a spirit of divination began to announce them as servants of the most high God. The enemy does this to win trust and validation of those with little or no sense of smell in the spirit. Jesus said, "You will know them by their fruits." What fruit do they produce in their lives and what is their message producing? Is it producing the fruit of the Spirit of love, joy and peace? Is it influencing godliness in others or is it producing chaos and darkness? Is it flowing from a heart of Father's love or from wrong motivations of the heart? These must be discerned by the Spirit.

Finally, you must test yourself. 1 Corinthians 11:28 say, "Let a man examine himself." Make sure you are living in surrender to the Lord, free from bitterness and other attitudes that contaminate the heart. Find a ministry that can help you find freedom from bondages, so you can minister out of wholeness. Every motivation of the heart must be tested by the Lord. God desires that we minister out of His love. Many people are very good at discerning everything and everybody but themselves. But they need to continually check themselves to make sure they are moving in the right spirit. Even in the natural people are continually checking their own odor to not be an offense to others; how much more should we be doing the same with our spiritual nose?

Many churches reject the gifts and manifestations of the Holy Spirit because they have never taught the people how to have a keen sense of smell. They haven't taught people to discern. Satan throws in a counterfeit and they reject the prophetic flow or other gifts altogether, just to be "safe."

Unfortunately they also throw out the legitimate move of God and are left with powerless ministry. As we move into the powerful times of outpouring and demonstration of the goodness of God, our spiritual sense of smell will become increasingly important.

Groups that don't teach discernment and maturity to their people end up "dumbing down" the gospel. As they attempt to avoid wrong spirits and false manifestations they fall into doctrinal error. With the best motivations, mind you, but error is error! They come up with convoluted scriptural interpretations that would seem to indicate that miracles and Holy Spirit manifestations are not for today. They want to keep their people safe from eating any deadly thing, so they end up with a starvation ration of stale crackers and stagnant water. No wonder people aren't very hungry and are looking for meetings that only last 45 minutes. They are missing out on the huge feast God has set for us.

CESSATIONISM AND SEMI-CESSATIONISM

Cessationism derives its name from the verb "to cease". It is the name of a doctrine which tries to explain why the gifts and manifestations of the Holy Spirit have ceased and are no longer valid today. Its doctrinal hinge point is found in 1 Corinthians 13: 8-10:

"Love never fails. But where there are prophecies, they will fail; where there are tongues, they will cease; where there is knowledge, it will vanish away. For we know in part and we prophesy in part. But when that which is perfect has come, then that which is in part will be done away."

Their interpretation of this verse is "when that which

is perfect has come" is the Bible, so miracles, tongues, prophecies, etc., have all ceased. They say that now we just need the Bible. Yes we need the Bible, but that is not what is being referred to here. It is referring to the kingdom of heaven coming in its fullness. Where no one will need to say, "Know the Lord," because all will know Him from the least to the greatest. (Jer. 31:34)

Contrary to this doctrine, Acts 1:4-8 teaches us that the empowerment of the Holy Spirit is necessary to become power-filled witnesses for reaching the ends of the earth. This phrase indicates geography but also implies chronology. Which of the original apostles ministered in your region? There are still many end of the earth regions that you and I will reach through the demonstrations of the power and the Holy Spirit. Viva Las Vegas!

The need for safety and freedom from error is much better served through teaching and training people in spiritual maturity through the activation and development of the spiritual senses. And while producing safety, we empower people for the fulfillment of the great commission.

BASIC REQUIREMENTS FOR DISCERNMENT

To be able to discern truth properly, you must be a born-again Christian, having an ongoing living relationship with the Lord Jesus Christ.

You should be baptized in the Holy Spirit, so you can sense from within what is truth. This should be evident by the manifestations of the Spirit including the manifestation of speaking in tongues.

You should have the spiritual senses activated to some

degree, especially the spiritual sense of hearing.

You must believe that the Bible is the Word of God. You should have a good understanding of the New Testament and be working on understanding the rest of the Bible.

You must be living a life that is surrendered to God's will. God's will is evident in the Scriptures and applied through hearing by the Spirit.

You should be in an accountable relationship with other mature Christians. As you relate with others, you can bounce things off of one another and discern what is right or wrong.

God desires His people to have spiritual smell and taste, not only to discern what is wrong, but to "taste and see that the Lord is good". He wants us to enjoy His goodness and His fragrance from heaven.

SPIRITUAL SENSE OF TOUCH

Spiritual touch is your largest sense, just as it is in the natural. In the natural you have nerve cells throughout your body that give a lot of information about where you are and how you're doing. Touch gives you a sense of your orientation, whether upright or reclining. And it also gives you a sense of your surroundings. I have experienced this many times as I come before the very throne of God during times of inspired worship or during intimate times of "soaking" in His presence.

I believe the main purpose of this sense is to make us aware when the presence of God is present or absent from our lives. At those time we begin to seek Him anew and we maintain our intimacy with the Lord. We should not have long periods of spiritual desert, where we no longer sense His closeness. Any sense of absence should lead us into a diagnostic mode: what has changed? Have I allowed some obstacle to come between us?

One time shortly after having surrendered to God's plan for my life, I became aware of this kind of absence. I was a teenager, but I had learned to know God's presence and it was definitely missing. On this particular Labor Day, I was spending a day of prayer and communion with the Lord and I felt so dry. "Lord, where are you?" I cried out.

Then the still, inner voice began to speak, "You have allowed cobwebs to separate you from me."

"Cobwebs? What does that mean?" I inquired.

"You have allowed your image of who you are to come between us," He said.

I knew what He was referring to. This was the era of the hippies and I was trying to identify with them. My hair and clothing were defining who I was. I came to an instantaneous resolve: All of that would have to go, because I would have nothing stand between me and Jesus. I turned to my older brother, Daniel and said, "Cut my hair!"

He said, "I don't know how to cut hair!" But he finally conceded to do it.

Did he ever prove it! By the time we kept trying to even out his errors, I basically had no hair left. Other items I was wearing went, too. I was no longer "cool", but I was bathed in the intimate love of Jesus. This was not about hair and clothes, it was about the state of my heart. The hair and clothes just happened to get in the line-of-fire of a passionate love for Jesus. I was taking the kingdom violently!

This ability to sense God's presence has marked my whole life. It has been like a compass that constantly indicates true north. Every believer needs this to navigate through life in a time when society has lost its foundational bedrock.

MINISTERING BY THE SENSE OF TOUCH

Spiritual touch is the ability to touch heaven and also touch others with the power of God. It is the ability to feel God's manifested presence and also the ability to sense what someone needs from God. Words of knowledge can come by feeling the pain of another person.

You can learn to feel the presence of the Lord and what He wants to do. Often I can sense in the Spirit that God wants do something special at a particular moment, so I've learned to go with it. That is the spiritual sense of touch. You can have physical sensations that go with this.

Some get the physical sensation of heat on their hands. That is often a demonstration that God wants to work through that person to another. He may want to bring healing or impartation. It is for action. These types of physical sensations can come when one is touched by the Holy Spirit.

When you touch heaven, the Holy Spirit can cause you to be carried by Him to other places. You can be translated in the Spirit and be taken somewhere else. Paul said this in Col. 2:5, "For though I am absent in the flesh, yet I am with you in spirit, rejoicing to see your good order and the steadfastness of your faith in Christ." He was telling them that he was not with them physically, but he was there in the

Spirit. He was not in touch with them by the natural man, but he was in touch with them by the Spirit.

I was in my prayer tent one day when I was transported in the Spirit. As I waited on God, I was caught up in the Spirit and began flying through the air. Soon I was flying over land and I could see rivers and mountains underneath me. I recognized where I was going. I was coming down the Huallaga River basin in a valley of the Andes Mountains in Peru. Then I landed in the city of Huanuco. I flew right into the house of one of our pastors there. (This pastor had recently called me to say that he had just been diagnosed with a heart problem and the doctor had told him if he didn't get out of ministry he was going to die.)

I "flew" right into his bedroom where he and his wife were asleep. I placed my hand on his heart and I proclaimed healing on his heart and a renewed excitement and vision in ministry. Then I walked around the bed to his wife. She was the lady who for fifteen days couldn't speak Spanish when she got baptized in the Holy Spirit. I placed my hand on her head and proclaimed that she would have a renewed experience with the Holy Spirit.

Later, I told Lynnie about my experience and she suggested we call the pastor in Peru to see if anything had happened. A couple of days later I called him and I asked, "Edgar, how is your heart?"

He said, "You know, it is the strangest thing. I woke up a couple of mornings ago and was perfectly fine. Just from one day to the next I was suddenly healed. I feel no effects, no problems."

"Well, what about Doris?" I asked.

He said that all of a sudden she had another dramatic

encounter with the Holy Spirit and was again speaking in tongues and couldn't speak any Spanish. (This lasted ten days.)

This was right after I had been in their house by the Spirit. I had prayed those prayers over them and then came back into the tent. My body had stayed in the tent, but I had been sent overseas in the Spirit.

I don't know how translation works but I don't have to know. I would say that for God to take me in the Spirit somewhere would be easier than doing it in body. It would be quicker than having to travel there by airplane.

We know that Philip was translated in his body in the book of Acts and was taken somewhere to bring someone to Jesus. That is the other kind of translation; it is a physical and bodily translation. If this occurred in the New Testament, it should not be strange for us today.

How does this apply to spiritual touch? In my experience I was touched by the Lord and was then able to touch someone else in the Spirit. You can extend the touch of God to others either physically or spiritually. These are things God does as we come to Him, spend time with Him and are touched by Him.

God wants to remove spiritual leprosy from the body of Christ. Leprosy is a disease that causes people to lose the ability to feel or sense touch. Therefore they cannot feel good sensations nor can they feel when they are being hurt. Damage comes to their body because of lack of feeling. But God wants to restore spiritual touch to the body of Christ.

Spiritual touch can flow by someone feeling heat or electricity, by a feeling of peace or by a flow of healing. Words of knowledge or healings often come through spiritual touch.

God wants our sense of touch to be activated so we can receive from Him and so we can extend His touch to others.

5

HINDRANCES TO SPIRITUAL SENSES

God wants us to flow in the spiritual senses and to be freed from blockages that keep us from receiving the initiatives of heaven. When you consistently avoid the things that hinder while at the same time you consistently do the things that activate the spiritual senses, you will have all the right conditions for the Spirit of God to move through you. You will become effective and fruitful in your particular arena of influence.

Let me give you a list of five obstacles to hearing the voice of the Lord, (or receiving through any of the spiritual senses). There may be other blockages that you discover, but here are five I know about.

CONDEMNATION

The first obstacle to hearing clearly from God is a condemned or a guilty heart. This is the heart that harbors un-repented sins. I believe sin has no power over us, except that which we give it. And where sin may still occupy a place in our hearts, it is simply that we have let that place be empty of God's grace.

Heb. 10:22 says, "Let us draw near with a true heart in full assurance of faith, having our hearts sprinkled from an evil conscience and our bodies having been washed with pure water."

James 4:8 says, "Draw near to God and He will draw near to you. Cleanse your hands, sinners; and purify your hearts, double-minded ones." When someone feels guilty, the enemy beats them down and it pulls them away from hearing God. They are too ashamed to come to God.

Sin is simple to take care of. One can quickly ask God for forgiveness from sin. 1 John 1:9 says, "If we confess our sins, He is faithful and just to forgive us our sins and to cleanse us from all unrighteousness." One needs to call it sin, not just a "mistake". Through confession and repentance, a person can be set free. Jesus will wash it clean by His shed blood. He is always waiting for us. When we allow Jesus to fill that place in our heart with something new, it will be life-giving. This will always involve some new actions that we begin to take.

True repentance comes through a process that we have called "replacement therapy". Exchanging sinful actions, for godly actions. Not religious actions, but "initiatives of heaven" actions.

As we draw near to God, we can command a spirit of condemnation to leave. We can come boldly to the throne of grace to find help in time of need. His grace is His power to move us beyond sin and guilt and into the flow of spiritual senses.

When someone has areas of ongoing sin in their heart and life, they are under a spirit of condemnation that causes hardness of heart and an inability to clearly hear from the Lord. They can hear from the Lord enough to bring them to repentance, but as far as hearing from God for daily decisions through an intimate walk with Him, guilt drives a wedge between that person and God.

As we turn from sin and turn to God, communication and directions are restored. The Lord begins to deal with deep-seated issues in our lives. We can respond by saying, "Lord, I give this to you right now. Deal with my heart because I want to hear from you." As sin and guilt is removed, suddenly we sense the Father's love and we can be freed to catch heavenly initiatives.

True repentance is not just feeling sorry, it is replacement therapy! You quit walking in the flesh and you walk in the Spirit. Galatians 5:16 says, "I say then: Walk in the Spirit and you shall not fulfill the lust of the flesh." As you walk in the Spirit, you are replacing the old with the new. You are doing His will instead of your own, as you listen and see and then say and do. It is catching the initiatives of heaven and doing the works of Jesus. This is true replacement therapy for sin, guilt and shame.

We had a young man in our church who fell into drug binges from time to time. He would call me and I would tell him to get back up and try walking right again. Finally one day when he called after having fallen again, I received an initiative from heaven for him. I told him that he should begin replacement therapy. He asked, "What is that?" I didn't know, so I asked the Lord, "What is that?" Then God revealed the truth to me.

I answered the young man, "When you want drugs, you need to go looking for it, don't you?" "Yes," he replied. "Well, from now on, when you have that desire and are about to go looking for the drugs, I want you to replace it by finding someone to talk to about Jesus at that moment." So he began doing just that!

Soon he was leading one person after another to the Lord. One day he said, "Lord, I need someone to talk to about you right now!"

Because he had learned about catching initiatives from heaven, the Lord said, "Stop your car and start honking your horn and I will bring people to you." So he obeyed.

He honked his horn and a group of children came and gathered around him, maybe thinking he was the ice cream man. He preached to them about Jesus and led them all in a prayer to receive Jesus into their hearts.

He walked to a nearby church and asked if they had a children's ministry that would disciple these kids. "No, but we would like one. If you come and teach them, then you can bring them." So this young man began a children's ministry, teaching these children to have spiritual senses activated to hear from God. He taught them how to minister healing and how to move in the prophetic. (One time the pastor came in to visit and all the children gathered around and prophesied over him!)

This young man continued reaching people for the Lord, at his job, among the homeless, on mission trips, all by catching initiatives from heaven. Once, he got the instruction from heaven to buy a box of oranges and give them away for free to some soccer players in Peru. He called them over saying, "Free oranges!" When they ran over to him, he said he just needed to say a few words first. He talked about Jesus and ended up leading the whole team to the Lord with a salvation prayer!

This young man is now a full-time missionary in another country and has led literally thousands to the Lord! Oh and by the way, when he began doing replacement therapy, walking in the power of Jesus instead of the flesh, all the desire for drugs dried up!

So condemnation of a guilty heart, can be healed by true repentance—by walking in the initiatives of heaven.

AN UNFORGIVING HEART

The next thing after condemnation that separates us from hearing God is an unforgiving heart. This is the heart that embraces offense. Matthew 6:14-15 says, "For if you forgive men their trespasses, your heavenly Father will also forgive you; but if you do not forgive men their trespasses, neither will your Father forgive your trespasses." A good way to walk in forgiveness is to release all those who have offended you to God, the only true judge of all.

Forgiveness does not mean you agree with what someone did. Many say they cannot forgive because they think it means endorsing what was done. But that is not the case at all. Forgiveness simply means that you surrender that offending person and that situation into the hands of the righteous judge. You are not the judge, He is and He will deal with that person and that situation when you let go.

As long as you don't forgive, you will live in torment. Matthew 18:34, 35 says, "And his master was angry and delivered him to the torturers until he should pay all that was due him. So My heavenly Father also will do to you if each of you, from his heart, does not forgive his brother his trespasses." The resulting torment can be spiritual, emotional or physical.

I have seen people delivered from all kinds of torment when they simply gave up the right to judge others. I have seen cases of physical illness healed as people forgave. I have seen financial torment reversed as people forgave. I have seen people who were under demonic control get set free as they forgave.

Forgiveness could mean going to the offending person

and working the situation out. Matthew 5:24 says, "leave your gift there before the altar and go your way. First be reconciled to you brother and then come and offer your gift." If reconciliation can occur by talking it over, that is great. But many times, the other person is not willing to reconcile or may have passed away. In that case, you can pull that person and that situation out of your heart and offer it to the Lord.

Even if you feel like the offending person does not deserve to be forgiven, yet you deserve to be free from the poison of bitterness. Forgiveness brings health to your soul and body and draws you back into relationship with God so you can hear Him. As you forgive, you are no longer controlled emotionally by a hurtful event or person. You are no longer stuck in time and you can move forward with freedom in life. If you choose not to forgive, it leads you down a path of torment and it blocks your ability to hear from God.

NINE DEADLY EMBRACES

The Lord spoke to me in a dream one night about nine deadly embraces as a strategy of the devil to lead people into bondage. In the dream I saw a man being freed from a destructive lifestyle and the Lord told me, "He is re-emerging from the nine embraces." I woke up and the Lord had me write the list.

EMBRACE OF AN OFFENSE

The first deadly embrace is the embrace of an offense. A person gets hurt and offended by someone for what they did or said. A spirit of offense comes on the heels of such an offensive event. The Bible says that offenses will come, but it is up to each one of us to either embrace the offense or release it immediately to God. If one embraces the spirit of offense, they have opened a door for other embraces to follow. This is a strategy of the enemy to bring people into bondage.

EMBRACING A LYING SPIRIT OF REINTERPRETATION

After the embrace of a spirit of offense, comes the embrace of a lying spirit of reinterpretation. The enemy blows the whole offense out of proportion and reinterprets the event. For example, "When he raised his eyebrows he meant this. And when he crossed his arms he meant that." It's a lying spirit that exaggerates events and explains things in a negative way. This usually happens after one walks away from the event and suddenly feels enlightened about actions and motives of the other person. It feels like discernment, but it is a lying spirit of reinterpretation that is being embraced.

EMBRACING A SPIRIT OF ACCUSATION AND JUDGMENT

Next comes the embrace of a spirit of accusation and judgment. A person criticizes and judges the motives of the heart of the person that offended them and accusations flow. The scripture is clear, "Judge not that you be not judged."

EMBRACING A SPIRIT OF BITTERNESS

Number four is the spirit of bitterness. The scripture warns about bitterness. Heb. 12:15 says, "Looking carefully lest anyone fall short of the grace of God; lest any root of bitterness springing up cause trouble and by this many become defiled." You can tell you are in bitterness when you relive the same event over and over in your mind. You feel the same emotions and then begin to spread it to others. The scripture warns of a spirit of bitterness, because it defiles many. It is poison. It's like responding with, I'll show them! I'll drink poison! And it brings you to torment. After you have embraced bitterness, scripture says in Matthew 18 that you are given over to the tormenters until such a time as you forgive. So now these tormentors have a right to lock you up and torment you. This is actually a transitional point. The first four points you choose to embrace. The following five points embrace you whether you want them to or not.

Transition from Embracing to Being Embraced!

Embraced by a Spirit of Deception

The fifth embrace is the spirit of deception. You become confused about who God is, who you are and about all truth in general. If you know the truth you will come to freedom, but the enemy's long term plan is to take you away from the truth through a spirit of deception. The spirit of deception leads you from the truth and keeps you locked up in deceptive belief systems and world-views.

Embraced by a Spirit of Fear and Depression

Number six is an embrace of a spirit of fear and depression. Unexplainable fears and depressions take place. A person just wants to hide away in depression. Fears come out of nowhere. They are uncontrollable. The embrace of a spirit of fear and depression takes over as further torment.

EMBRACED BY A SPIRIT OF COMPULSIONS, OBSESSIONS AND ADDICTIONS

The seventh is an embrace of a spirit of compulsions, obsessions and addictions. This can include an addiction to pornography or drugs or an unhealthy obsession towards another person or even compulsive hand-washing. It can be something destructive or it can even look religious. It can look good. Some people compulsively fast, but they feel compelled to do so. It is not the leading of the Spirit, it is a demonic spirit. Obsessions, compulsions and addictions are taskmasters.

EMBRACED BY A SPIRIT OF CONTROL

Number eight is a spirit of control. This spirit not only controls a person, but controls others through them. Manipulative control and dominative control has many masks. It can manifest through flattery, through tears, through shouting or through subtle manipulation. It can come through passive control, such as "I may get really sick if you don't do what I want," or through aggressive control which dominates and controls. This is the embrace of a spirit of control.

EMBRACED BY A SUPPRESSING SPIRIT

Number nine is suppression of identity. A person's identity begins to be suppressed by a demonic spirit that embraces the person. The words and actions are no longer theirs, but are caused by a spirit moving through them. This is the final level of nine demonic, deadly embraces.

NOW THE GOOD NEWS

The good news about all this is that the Lord told me that if you find someone who is stuck in any of those stages, all you have to do is take them back to the original offense and deal with that. When they release number one, the offending people and events, all the house of cards that the enemy has erected falls to the ground. We have seen cases where people were demonically oppressed at number nine. All we did was allow the Holy Spirit to show where offense came in. As they released it all to the Lord, freedom came.

We were in Ecuador and a young lady came forward to give her heart to the Lord in one of our meetings. We started praying for her and she fell to the floor manifesting demonic spirits. She was writhing, spitting and manifesting spirits of lust. Some ladies from that church rushed to her, held her down and began shouting, "The blood of Jesus!" The commotion grew, but I felt to continue ministering to people in the prayer line.

As I was ministering to the last person in line, the Lord gave me two words of knowledge for the girl who was still in torment. Right then my brother-in-law, Jim Drown, came over and said, "Dennis, can you do something with her? They haven't gotten anywhere." So I walked over and asked the ladies if they wouldn't mind leaving us alone with her, so they agreed and left.

I looked at the girl and said, "Look at me!" Still under the influence of demons, she closed her eyes and wouldn't look at me. Then I spoke to the girl, "If you don't work with me, I am going to have to leave you like you are." She struggled and opened her eyes and looked at me. In a small plaintive voice she said, "Don't leave me. I need help." I now knew that she could work with me. God had led me to do this. This was an initiative from heaven. Then I spoke the words of knowledge I had received.

I asked her, "What did your father do that you have to forgive?" That was the first word of knowledge—that she had to forgive her father. She struggled and finally admitted that her father had abandoned her family when she was seven years of age and they had never seen him again. So I asked her, "Can you forgive him? Can you give him up to God?" She struggled a bit and finally nodded. She could forgive her father.

Next I asked, "Who was the man who sexually abused you as a child?" That was the second word of knowledge I had received—that she had been sexually abused as a child. She began crying and said, "I'm not bad. I'm not bad." I looked at her and said, "No, you are not bad and I take authority over the spirit of condemnation that has told you that all of this is your fault. So right now I command it to go! Who was the man?" She had to struggle to answer me. Finally she told me that her mom had remarried a year later. At eight years of age her step-father had begun to sexually abuse her. I asked her, "Can you give him up to God, too? Can you forgive him and give him over to the hands of the just judge? You are not the judge; God is the judge of all. If you will give him to God and let God be the judge, you will be free." She finally nodded her head.

I had her put her hands together like a cup and I began to take things out of her heart and put them in her hands. The Lord led me to do that. I took her father out of her heart and put him in her hands. I took the other man out, her step-father and put him in her hands. All the abuse, all the abandonment, blame towards her mother and other things that the Lord showed me by word of knowledge, I pulled out of her heart and put in her hands.

Finally I said, "This is now in your power to do with as you want. I suggest that you give it all to God." This is important, as many feel powerless in these kinds of situations. By putting it all in her hands, it was a demonstration that she now had power over it to do with as she would. She agreed, so I helped her raise her cupped hands to the Lord. She struggled against the demons and repeated after me, "Lord, I am not the judge, you are the only true and righteous judge and I give you all these people, all these events and all these emotions. I release them to you."

When she spread her lifted hands, offering it all to the Lord, she was strongly shaken as there was an absolute deliverance taking place. We looked at her a moment later and saw God's peace come over her.

We were waiting on God, asking, "Is there anything else?" Jim leaned over to me as he received a word from the Lord. "She has had thoughts of suicide." So I asked her in Spanish, "Have you had thoughts of killing yourself?" She nodded yes. So I asked the Lord about it and He said, "You have already dealt with the underlying issues that gave it a right to be there. Just tell it to go." So I commanded the spirit of suicide to come off. She shook again and we sensed it leave.

A sense of total peace came over her. Jim leaned toward me and said, "She sees Jesus right now." So I asked her in Spanish, "Do you see Jesus right now?" With her eyes closed, she nodded her head, smiling, saying, "He loves me. He loves me." She had the love of Jesus being ministered to her by Jesus Himself. She was filled with His love. We told her, "You will continue to remain free if you continue to give up to the Lord all those thoughts and emotions related to those past events. The devil will try to get you to embrace offense again, but you will not do it! You have learned how to live in freedom. Go home and continue your relationship with God. Come to the church, be faithful."

The next day she came back to the meeting and brought her whole family—her mom, her brother and her sister. Each one of them gave their heart to the Lord. Her whole family was born again. And she was sitting there with a huge "Colgate" grin across her face.

Later she told us that she had been living with the compulsion to have sex with absolute strangers and then she would feel so ashamed and dirty. Finally she had come to such a depression that she wanted to end her life. On her way to end her life, she decided to give God a last chance that night by coming into the church she was passing by. If nothing changed, she would still end her life. God had truly intervened in her life!

We kept up with that family and they continue to serve faithfully in the church. In an evangelistic healing crusade in their city, where I was translating for Todd Bentley, she was one of the ushers. We saw her and gave her a hug. Her life had been changed forever by the power and love of God.

Forgiveness sets a person free to hear from God and follow His destiny for their life. The nine deadly embraces' downward spiral begins with an unforgiving heart which blocks the ability to hear God. But you can receive the initiatives of heaven to set people free. If you see someone in any one of those stages, you can be an agent of the Lord to set them free. You can help them find the original offense, maybe by a word of knowledge and help them release it all to the Lord. Then command all attached spirits to leave. Then pray that the Father's love fill the void.

The spiritual senses flow again when forgiveness comes so one can catch initiatives from heaven.

PRIDE AND PRESUMPTION

Another issue that can keep you from hearing God is pride or presumption. As soon as you think you really are something, then God resists you. James 4:6 says, "God resists the proud, but gives grace to the humble." As soon as you think you know how to do everything without God's help, you are walking in pride or presumption and apart from God's presence.

One of the main enemies of the miracle power of God is powerless, pointless and *presumptuous* prayer. We pray like we have it all figured out. Jesus never did that. When He ministered healing to blind Bartimaeus, He didn't pray, "Oh Father, I know that You said in Your scripture that none of these diseases that came on the Egyptians will come on us. I claim this healing in my name!" Many people preach at God in prayer! They get very wordy. They get religious. But Jesus did not do that to minister healing. He just followed His Father's directions from heaven and miracles occurred.

There is a time for prayer and petition, but then there is a time for ministering healing. There is a time for preaching, but when it is time to heal the sick, it is not time for those things. That is when it is time to expect to catch a heavenly initiative for healing.

Yes, you can prime the pump for a flow of thoughts inspired by the Holy Spirit by beginning with what you know from the Word of God, but then you must flow into what you don't know. You must have ears attuned to what Jesus is doing right now. This applies whether you speak a prophecy over someone or for ministering healing. You can start with God's *logos* written Word, but then you must flow into God's *rhema* spontaneous Word from heaven. You can start by saying, "God loves you," based on the written Word of God, but then you must flow into the initiatives of heaven. Jesus is working right now.

Jesus said in John 14:12, "Most assuredly, I say to you, he who believes in Me, the works that I do he will do also; and greater works than these he will do, because I go to My Father." Notice it says the works that I do, not the works that I did. He is moving in present tense. He wants you to see and hear and move with Him in your present situation, catching the initiatives of heaven.

God hates sickness and death and His will is always to set people free, but He doesn't want us moving in formulas or habits. God's number one priority for our lives is that we would know Him, but He also wants to deliver us from all our afflictions. Moving by the initiative of heaven accomplishes both of these things. You learn to know God as His power is flowing through you because of the initiatives of heaven you have caught and obeyed. In the process, healings, deliverances, miracles, salvations and transformations occur. It is about hearing instructions from heaven and working with the Father. That is what Jesus did.

Jesus related with the Father by seeing and hearing Him, walking in communion and relationship with Him. Relationship is what He is drawing you into. He wants you to see, to hear and to interact with heaven. Using computer jargon, He wants you to interface with heaven and get the downloads from heaven. The purposes and plans of God are not just to heal someone, but to develop you as His child and to bring you into closer relationship. That is probably more important than a single healing, but it doesn't lessen the fact that God hates illness. He hates sickness and He hates death. It is always His will to see people healed, but He wants to bring us into a place where we are relating to Him, where we are hearing and seeing and following and catching the initiatives of heaven.

RESIST PRESUMPTION

Sometimes we don't see someone healed, but I still feel it's all about relationship. I love to see someone healed, but if I don't see it happen, it means I need to get closer to Him. I need to see what is going on. I need more of His thoughts, more of His reasons. Or it could be as simple as this: *that* healing didn't belong to me (for me to perform). Jesus didn't always heal everyone. Remember the lame man who sat at the gate of the temple in Jerusalem for forty years? Jesus must have passed by him more than once, but *that* healing was reserved for Peter and John after Jesus was caught up to heaven. It became the spark that ignited revival in Jerusalem.

The truth is that God does not want everyone looking to me or running to me. He wants people to look to Him and run to Him. That is why He is activating the body of His believers to do these things—not just a few! How many healings are we missing because not everyone is ready to do these works? Pride and presumption will push you into trying to do something Jesus is not telling you to do. To pray without relating to Him.

The greatest obstacle to moving by the Spirit and receiving His initiative, is a natural good idea or a religious action that replaces a living connection with the Holy Spirit. Jesus did not do that. He said, "I only do what I see my Father in heaven do." Every need here on earth is an opportunity for the power of God to transform it by an initiative of heaven. But when we fill that opportunity with something less than what comes by the initiative of heaven, we lose the opportunity for God to be glorified on earth. People often times have allowed blockages to interfere with the ability of their spiritual senses to function. So they fall back on repetitive weak and pusillanimous (small-spirited) prayers.

Have you ever noticed that most of our prayers follow the same pattern—they start and end the same with just a little change of content. Is it any wonder that these kinds of prayers don't carry much weight? In contrast, Jesus never prayed these kind of prayers. You see Jesus catching the initiatives of His Father in heaven and acting or commanding based on those instructions. The way to break out of this habit of one-size-fits-all prayers is to consciously step back and look to heaven before launching out in prayer. But sometimes that is not enough by itself; you need to deal with the blockages to the spiritual senses.

Jesus had such an intimate relationship with the Father that He didn't run ahead or lag behind what the Father was doing. He was there waiting and listening and hearing the Father. He was close to Him. He was not presumptuous. He was not fearful.

In fact, Jesus said some things to turn people away and

offend them. When you say to a Jew, "Unless you eat my flesh and drink my blood you have no part with me," you can't get more offensive than that. That happened right after the crowds were about to take Him and forcibly make Him king.

I think this falls into the category of WWJND. What Would Jesus Not Do? Jesus was not about to be made king by earthly initiatives. He was going to be made king by the initiative of heaven, not the initiative of earth. When they were going to take the initiative on earth to make Him king, He did whatever He could to bring offense to that spirit and to push them away and it worked. People were not hearing or understanding by the Spirit.

Jesus spoke words that were not understood. The Pharisees and unbelievers had no idea what He was talking about. They were offended by what He said and suddenly left Him. He then asked His disciples, "Will you also leave me?" And they responded, "Where would we go? You have the words of life." They chose to do things His way, not their own, even when it made no sense. Pride will cause us to do things in our own reasoning. And as we all know, God's ways are not our ways! So natural understanding can hinder us from flowing in spiritual senses.

Pride goes with presumption, because it believes it can be done without God's help. It even believes that God's ways are too foolish. In 1 Corinthians 2:14, it says that the natural man cannot receive the things of the Spirit, for they are foolishness to him, neither can he know them, for they are spiritually discerned. In the Old Testament, when King David danced before the Lord with all his might, his wife, in her pride, said he was being foolish before everyone. He responded that he would be even more foolish if necessary. It is interesting that she became barren and had no children. A heart of pride cannot bear fruit. It is dead religion.

A prideful heart does not understand broken humility and isn't open to hearing God. It is a heart that runs from the breakings and dealings of the Lord. But God says in Luke 20:18, "Whoever falls on that stone will be broken; but on whomever it falls, it will grind him to powder."

God will allow you to fall on your face in order to break the pride. The picture I get is of an inflated balloon, but God has the right little sticker, thistle or whatever it takes to pop that balloon. I had a situation occur one time that illustrates this.

BEWARE OF DITCHES

Years ago, while living as a young missionary in Peru, we were getting lots of rain. The streets of the city were flooded with about six or eight inches of water, even running into the stores. An acquaintance came and asked me to drive him around. I had a car that was loaned to me, but he wanted me to be his personal chauffeur to drive him around to do all his personal shopping. I got rather upset at that. I thought, "I am a preacher of the Word. I could be doing something more important than being a taxi driver. I could be at home right now writing a sermon on love or something like that." Besides, this guy had a reputation of spending too much time in auto parts stores and hardware stores. One of the places he wanted me to take him was a car repair shop. He wanted to look for parts. I was not happy about this, but agreed to take him.

I drove him there, but not with a good attitude. I parked

out front while he went in. I waited and waited. Fifteen minutes, thirty minutes, forty-five minutes went by and finally I got to the end of my patience. I thought, "I am going to march in there, grab him, pull him out and drop him off somewhere and go home."

I went marching in through the big double doors where the cars and trucks were pulled in to be repaired. All the workers were lined up against the wall. There was no business because the water had invaded their shop. I had my big rubber boots on to walk through water. I marched in and they all started snickering at me and pointing. I thought, "What is the deal?" I checked myself to see if someone had put a sign on me, but nothing. They laughed even harder, until I stepped and fell into a water-filled ditch.

In Peru, they don't have lifts, they have ditches where they go underneath the trucks to work on them and it was covered in water. They knew I was headed right for it. I took one final step, received an absolute baptism and came out covered in greasy, dirty water. I must have look like a mess. If I was mad before, now I was absolutely burning mad. I stormed out, thinking, "I am leaving that turkey behind."

I jumped into the car and put it into gear and drove it right into another ditch! The whole front of the car was under water. Fortunately it was a Volkswagen so the engine was in the back. Still, there was water almost up to the windshield. Twenty seconds and two ditches! I was really upset and began crying out to God, "You are supposed to protect me. I am your servant. Why two ditches in twenty seconds? Why?" Then the Lord told me why.

He showed me my attitude—my thoughts. It replayed before me and He showed me how proud I had gotten. This was just what I needed to deflate all that pride. There I was sitting soaking wet, dirty, filthy and greasy, in a car stuck in the water. I began to pray and ask God to forgive me. "God forgive me of my pride. Deal with this."

I have learned that the way to embrace a breaking is to ask God what to do to complete the work. So I asked God, "What do I do right now?" The Lord spoke to me, "Go back into the shop and ask all the workers to come and help you pull out the car." I would much rather have called a tow truck or someone on the street to help pull me out. But I obeyed and went in to ask for their help.

When the guys came out and saw the car in the water, it looked like they were having heart attacks laughing at me. I had fallen into one ditch and then I had driven into another. I became famous in the city. Every time I walked by that place, they would laugh all over again. After that, every time I walked by a ditch I would check my heart. I would think, "How is my heart today? Is there pride here?"

The Lord knows how to perform the breakings that work well for us. He knows how to deal with pride and presumption in our lives so we can hear from Him more clearly.

As we live in humility and surrender, in relationship with Him, we can catch initiatives from heaven to bring miracles to earth.

A FEARFUL HEART

Fear is a fourth area that can keep us from hearing God. In Judges 7:3 it says, "Gideon let all the fearful depart from facing war and 22,000 went home."

Abraham was called by God to follow Him, even though He didn't tell him where he was going. He had to leave his father, conquering fear, to become the father of faith.

Fear can paralyze you from stepping out on what you're hearing. If He has spoken for you to do or say something and you are afraid to take the risk to move on it, then it may block your ability to hear from God again. The Lord continues to speak and is patient, but He is looking for someone to follow through on what He is saying. To hear and obey.

The Bible says we see in part, we know in part, we prophesy in part. You might as well resolve that you are going to make mistakes, so go ahead and get all your mistakes out of the way at once. Go to Walmart where no one in church knows you or sees you and try it out. Ask God to give you initiatives or prophetic messages for the people you meet. If you make mistakes, no one at church will ever know! But you might get it right. That's how you grow. If you let fear overcome you, it will rob you of your ability to grow and hear from God. Short-term mission trips are also a good arena for learning; any mistakes will be left far away in just a few days. But the successes will be good seed for the great harvest.

As you overcome fear and move out in boldness, you will begin to grow in catching the initiatives of heaven. You will start getting more right than you get wrong. The little consequences of our puny mistakes are nothing in comparison with the glory that comes when you get it right!

DISTRACTED HEART

The fifth area that can keep you from hearing God is a distracted heart. This is the heart that has no time for God.

Heb. 3:10 says, "They always go astray in their heart." Distractions can keep us from hearing from the Lord. Our modern lives are so full of distractions. We have televisions, computers, jobs, sports, phones and various activities that keep our minds busy. They are not bad in themselves unless they are filling time we should have with our Lord.

Even as we fulfill our daily responsibilities in life, we must learn to listen to the Lord. It should be like having an antenna up to be aware of what the Spirit would say to us at all times no matter what we are doing. We must learn to intentionally hear from God in times set apart for Him alone, as well as keeping our senses attuned to Him throughout the day. God wants you to have a singleness of vision and a singleness of heart—a heart stayed on God.

I used to hear from God a lot in the shower. I would get in my shower and start soaping up and God would speak to me. I began to wonder why and the Lord showed me it was because I had no distractions there. No radio, television, phones, people, newspaper, computers, etc.

We must not allow the cares and distractions of life to keep us from hearing Him. He loves spending time with His people and wants to be in communication with us. We have a need to hear His voice so we can live our destiny to the fullest.

As we ignore distractions and focus on the promptings of

the Holy Spirit throughout the day, we can catch initiatives from heaven, bringing blessings into every area of our lives.

When I began spending time with God in my tent I was specifically dealing with distractions. I would zip up my tent, effectively dealing with visual distractions, then I would put on my earphones with instrumental music, dealing with the audible distractions. I would spend hours in that place learning to focus my mind on the things of heaven (Col. 3:2) and in this way I was dealing with the mental and spiritual distractions. The result of all this was a change in my character and an increase of the power of heaven being demonstrated in my life.

I know that anyone who will deal with the distractions and obey Colossians 3:1-2 will have similar results. Here is what it says:

"If then you were raised with Christ, seek those things which are above, where Christ is, sitting at the right hand of God. Set your mind on things above, not on things on the earth."

AWARENESS OF HEAVEN

As you deal with all the hindrances to the spiritual senses and press into the Spirit, you will become more and more aware of the kingdom of heaven. Jesus walked the earth but was constantly aware of the kingdom of heaven. He consistently walked in the initiatives of heaven, seeing and hearing His Father in heaven giving instructions for the needs at hand. He preached the kingdom of heaven and He demonstrated the kingdom of heaven. His central theme and the very purpose for His coming to earth was for the rejoining of heaven and earth. If you really want to know Jesus you will know the kingdom of heaven.

6

THE REJOINING OF HEAVEN AND EARTH

To fully understand the kingdom of heaven, you must understand that heaven and earth were never meant to be separated. In fact, they were created to be joined as one. This is clearly demonstrated in the first chapters of Genesis. In the garden of Eden, you see heaven and earth joined together.

In the garden of Eden, you see heavenly trees and earthly trees. The Tree of Life was not an earthly tree, nor was the Tree of the Knowledge of Good and Evil. That is why we no longer have them on earth. In Genesis 2:9, it mentions that God also caused trees to grow up from the ground. They were earthly trees. So there were earthly trees and heavenly trees.

In the garden there were four rivers, two of which we still have today, the Euphrates and Tigris. They were earthly rivers. Two other rivers have completely disappeared. One of those was a river that flowed through the land of Havilah where there was an abundance of gold. These rivers were heavenly rivers that we no longer have with us. So there were earthly rivers and heavenly rivers.

In the garden of Eden there were earthly beings and heavenly beings. God walked and talked with man in the garden. Adam himself was a joining of heaven and earth. He was formed from the dust of the earth and he was also God-breathed. He was spiritually alive until sin entered. And through one man's sin, spiritual death came upon all mankind (Rom. 5:12).

In that sad instance of disobedience, death came upon Adam and Eve. But God in His great love for mankind, postponed judgment. He split heaven and earth apart, since no sin or death can abide in God's presence in heaven. He had to quarantine man on earth, left alive physically, but devoid of the life of heaven. This was not because God was angry, but it was an act of mercy. Paul in Romans 8 says that the creation was subjected to futility (read death), not willingly, but in hope. That hope was of the coming Redeemer who by His own shed blood would accomplish the rejoining of heaven and earth for all those who believe in Him.

Jesus was the first man since Adam who was born with a living spirit. And He did not just have the same life Adam had before sin entered. He was far superior! Adam had a living (God-breathed) soul, but Jesus came to earth with a life-giving Spirit. He is the resurrection and the life—the One who joins heaven and earth through His unique conception. He was conceived when the Holy Spirit overshadowed Mary. He was born of man and born of God, re-uniting heaven and earth.

Jesus went all over Judea and Samaria demonstrating the heaven-initiated works of His Father, giving new life to all who believed in Him. He proclaimed and demonstrated that the kingdom of heaven had truly come to earth. The fullness of the kingdom was reserved for a future event, yet was brought to earth wherever a healing or miracle occurred. Jesus was the connector of heaven and earth.

HEAVEN COMES TO EARTH

God is bringing us to a place where we are seeing into heaven—we are being made more aware of heaven. We are coming into a place where God's grace and mercy are being so poured out that we can see evidences of the realities of heaven. He is calling us—inviting us. Matthew 7:7 says,

"Ask and it will be given to you; seek and you will find; knock and it will be opened to you." There are things that He has designed to be found by us. He is inviting and encouraging us to come into heavenly experiences.

There are things in this world that need to be overcome. Change needs to occur in areas of our lives, our neighborhoods, our country and our world. Not only bad areas, but things that seem innocuous and don't look so evil. These are actually voids which the absence of heaven has left on earth and it includes people who have lived entire lifetimes separated from God's love and grace. In heaven there is no sickness, sin, pain or death and when heaven comes to earth those things are overcome!

Whatever need we encounter on earth, God has that which will overcome it—that which is birthed in heaven and brought to earth (1 John 5:4). That is part of the reason why Jesus said to pray this way, "Our Father which art in heaven … Thy kingdom come, Thy will be done on earth as it is in heaven." We are supposed to catch the direction and the will of the Father and bring that to earth. These are the initiatives of heaven. We can catch the actions and words that God initiates in heaven and bring them to earth.

HEAVEN TRUMPS EARTH

1 John 5:4 has two relevant parts. The first part says, "That which is born of God overcomes the world." It could be translated "whosoever is born of God overcomes the world." But I like "that which is born of God" because it is talking about God's initiatives, God's directions and the words that

are birthed out of His mouth that overcome the world. He wants to bring us His ideas, His initiatives, His directives and His thoughts, in order to bring them to earth. This is the "that which" is born from God and when these kinds of things come to earth, whatever problem exists in the world is overcome. This is how He conveys His resources from heaven to earth.

Earth and Heaven—Created to Overlap

When God created Adam and Eve they were created with an ability to interface with the natural creation in the garden of Eden and with the spiritual creation that was visible to them at the same time. There was no division between the things of heaven and earth. You can see Adam and Eve walking and moving and talking with God in the garden and having communion with Him in the garden. They saw the Tree of Life there and the Tree of the Knowledge of Good and Evil along with the other trees that sprang forth from the ground and grew like natural trees. Heaven and earth were created to fit together in a harmonious fashion.

I believe that heaven and earth existed as one whole. And there is evidence in scripture that this is where we are heading again. The Apostle Paul declares that in the end Jesus will rejoin those things in heaven and on earth.

Ephesians 1:10 says "That in the dispensation of the fullness of the times He might gather together in one all things in Christ, both which are in heaven and which are on earth—

in Him."

In the end of the Book of Revelation, John saw the heavenly city, the New Jerusalem descending from heaven to the earth. Heaven is coming to earth and when we see signs and wonders occur, this is evidence of God's love and power invading earth. It is a prophetic sign of things to come, the kingdom of heaven coming to earth.

We are seeing cross-over manifestations that are evidences of the spiritual realm manifesting in the natural realm. Gold dust appears when the presence of God is manifest. Jewels appear out of nowhere. Limbs grow out where there were none. And the dead are raised. The power of heaven comes to earth! We are called to be the connectors of that reality to earth as we activate our spiritual senses.

When I was a kid I thought heaven was on one of the clouds floating overhead. I learned all the Sunday School lessons that we are going to be like angels in heaven playing harps, dressed in white and floating on clouds. I didn't even know if I wanted to go to heaven, but it was because I had wrong assumptions about heaven. But now I don't see heaven as some other planet. I don't see heaven as some other geographical place. I see heaven as being right here but on a different plane.

Remember, heaven and earth were together in the garden of Eden at creation, but when sin came, it was pulled apart. When Adam and Eve sinned they died spiritually and they died to heaven. Scripture says that Jesus came to seek and save that which was lost, in Luke 19:10. Now most of the time when we looked at that verse, we only looked at it from the perspective of what God lost. He lost communion with humanity and intimate relationship with humanity. He came to seek and save those who were lost, but that verse actually says "that which was lost" which includes our loss of heaven.

So from our perspective, what did we lose when heaven and earth were split apart and when Adam and Eve sinned? We lost an eternal life—body, soul and spirit—that had no sin and no sickness. We lost communion with God. We lost a life with God in heaven. We lost all the benefits of heaven. But Jesus came to seek and save that which was lost for God and also to seek and save that which was lost for you.

Ephesians 1:10 says that Jesus came to unite in one all those things in heaven and in earth in Him. I believe that the process and the plan of God is to reunite heaven and earth and to reunite creation. Scripture says that all creation groans and travails for the manifestation of the sons of God. It is groaning and travailing in order to have heaven restored to earth. I believe the whole natural creation is in pain and death, until such time as heaven and earth are rejoined through God's sons who catch the initiatives of heaven.

Jesus—Bi-Dimensional in Heaven and Earth

Jesus told Nicodemus what it means to see heaven and what it means to enter into heaven. We have put experiencing heaven off to some future event, either when we die or when the Lord returns. But Jesus didn't wait to die to go to heaven. In John 3:13 He was standing before Nicodemus saying, "Right now I am in heaven." He said that no one had ascended to heaven but he who descended, the son of man who is in heaven. Jesus' testimony was that He was in heaven right then while walking the streets of Jerusalem and Judea. He was the bi-dimensional new creation man living in the heavenly and earthly planes at the same time.

Jesus was in Jerusalem on earth, yet He was telling Nicodemus He was in heaven! "... the Son of Man who is in heaven." I believe this heavenly ascension occurred when He was baptized in water and the Spirit came on Him in the form of a dove. He was both water and Holy Spirit baptized at once. Immediately the heavens opened and God's voice spoke from heaven saying, "This is my Son in whom I am well pleased." (Luke 3:22). Jesus ascended to heaven in the Spirit and began living in heaven and on earth at the same time! From that point on, He began moving in miracles. He was led by the Holy Spirit into the wilderness and then into a life of signs and wonders. No miracles were performed before this experience. Later, after His death and resurrection, His body would also be taken to heaven for a bodily ascension into heaven.

The day before His first miracle, Jesus told Nathanael, in John 1:51, "You shall see heaven open and the angels of God ascending and descending upon the Son of Man."

The very next verse in John 2:1 says, "The next day..." and tells us the story of the miracle at Cana of Galilee. Heaven was opened and came to earth through Jesus as He received the initiatives of heaven.

Jesus was the heavenly man come to earth in order to unite heaven and earth. You can say that "His head was in the clouds and His feet were on the ground." His direction came from heaven and He lived it out on earth. Everything that Jesus did was initiated from heaven. That was His very testimony. He said nothing but what He heard His Father in heaven say. Jesus had His ears attuned to heaven, to the voice of the Father.

He said that man will not live by bread alone but by every word that comes from the mouth of God. That was His lifestyle—His ears were attuned to the words from heaven. Jesus asked the disciples at one point if they would leave Him and they said, "How could we leave you? You are the one who has the words of life." They were aware that the words He was speaking were not just thoughts or philosophies; they were not just cool lessons. He was not simply a great teacher, He was the man from heaven living on earth who dispensed life in every word that He spoke. His words were life-giving. They said, "You have the words of life." It so impressed them, that they could not ever imagine leaving Him, because He was the one who spoke the words of life. But it went beyond His words, even to His actions and His deeds.

Help from heaven came to earth when Jesus performed His first miracle. It came when He healed the sick, raised the dead, cleansed the lepers and preached the good news of this new kingdom dispensation.

WE ARE BI-DIMENSIONAL

We are commissioned to do the same works in Matthew 10:7, 8 as disciples of Jesus. We are to preach the gospel, heal the sick, raise the dead, cleanse the lepers and cast out demons. We are to live out of our "spirit man" which is already in heaven. The scripture says in Colossians 3:3, "For you died and your life is hidden with Christ in God."

Present tense, "is hidden". Our spirit is saved and perfect in heaven. Our spirit can't be more holy than it is right now in heaven.

Our soul is still being worked on and we are told to work out our own salvation with fear and trembling (Philippians 2:12). This comes through daily surrender to His Spirit. Character issues are being transformed daily.

Our body will yet be saved, "…in a moment, in the twinkling of an eye…" our bodies will be transformed, to show forth God's full salvation for us, body, soul and spirit.

So if we are seated with Christ in heavenly places (Col. 3) and our bodies are here are earth, then we are bi-dimensional beings.

We have a tremendous responsibility to be the conduits of heaven's power here to earth. Yet we often walk oblivious to this, simply living a natural life. The Lord wants us to grow in the exercise of the spiritual senses so we can catch things from heaven and impart them to earth so miracles can occur.

Jesus said in John 3:8, "The wind blows where it wishes and you hear the sound of it, but cannot tell where it comes from and where it goes. So is everyone who is born of the Spirit."

We become "wind people" when we are led by the Spirit. It says, "The wind blows … so is everyone who is born of the Spirit." We become children of heaven as we are blown here and there by the Spirit, doing His works. We are to follow Jesus' example of living by the Spirit and living from the initiatives of heaven. As we do, we will see transformations wherever we go.

Jesus Received Initiatives from Heaven

The power and life of heaven always overcomes the laws of the natural creation. "Whatever is born of God overcomes the world." (1 John 5:4) Whatever God instructs us to do here and now overcomes earth's natural laws. That's why Jesus could walk on water and thus overcome natural gravity. He could calm the storm, demonstrating power over the natural weather. He could pay taxes with a gold coin found in the fish's mouth, tapping into heavenly provision. Some think the provision was found in the fish's mouth, but actually it was found in Jesus' mouth. As He spoke the word from heaven and someone acted on it, the miracle happened. Man shall not live by bread alone but by every word proceeding from the mouth of God. Our provision comes at our obedience to His word. At our obedience to the initiative of heaven.

Have you ever taken five thousand people out to eat? Jesus did. He was not limited to natural resources or provision. He had tapped into heaven. He was looking into heaven to see what the Father was doing so He could flow with His plan. Notice the food didn't just fall out of the sky. Jesus received an initiative from heaven using something that was already on hand—a little boy's lunch. God likes to partner with mankind and get him involved in the miracle. Jesus blessed it, broke it and had the disciples feed it to the five thousand. A small action and a small amount of food in comparison to an immense need. But when you do what He's doing in heaven, even if it is a small action, the miracle occurs.

BIBLICAL CONTEXT

In the time that Jesus was on the earth, the Jews understood what it meant for the kingdom of heaven to come, because they had been taught that a Messiah and His kingdom would one day come and free them from the bondage they were living under. The prophecies stated that every tear would be wiped away and sorrow and mourning would flee away. These prophecies are found through out the Old Testament, but in their limited understanding, they thought this Messiah would come with an army and free them from the oppressive Roman rule.

Jesus came and healed the sick, raised the dead, cast out demons and preached saying, "The kingdom of heaven is at hand." He did not come in the way that was expected, with an army to overthrow those who ruled them, but in a much higher dimension. He came to free the whole world of slavery to sin, sickness and bondage to Satan and eventually even death.

In the garden of Eden, at the time of creation, God had given authority over the earth to Adam and Eve. Through temptation and sin, man had lost that authority and it was given over to Satan. Through the death and resurrection of Jesus, He took the authority back. He came to establish His kingdom here on earth.

That's why Jesus could say, "If I cast out demons by the Spirit of God, surely the kingdom of God has come upon you." (Matt. 12:28). In other words, as He freed people from Satan's bondage, He was establishing the dominion of a new kingdom.

Jesus won the ultimate victory over Satan through His

death and resurrection. His sacrifice paid the debt for the sin of mankind which had caused them to lose their authority in the beginning. He won the authority back!

Jesus told His disciples in Matt. 28, "All authority in heaven and on earth has been given to me, therefore go and make disciples of all nations, baptizing them in the name of the Father and of the Son and of the Holy Spirit, teaching them to observe all that I have commanded you."

He took the authority back from Satan, gave the keys back to mankind and told them to go spread His kingdom rule throughout the world by making disciples of all nations. He said in Matthew 16:19 "And I will give you the keys of the kingdom of heaven and whatever you bind on earth will be bound in heaven and whatever you loose on earth will be loosed in heaven." Jesus told us we can bind the work of sin and Satan and we can release healings, blessings and restoration here on earth. We can loose people from their bondage to sin and death. Jesus asks us to enforce His rule which He has already won.

How to Do Kingdom Works

Jesus walked around Judea doing miracles and healing the sick. He did these works, not out of His divinity, but as a man. Many people feel that Jesus did these works as the Son of God through His own divine power, but He made it clear in John 5:19, "… the Son can do nothing of Himself …" This may seem like trivial theology, but thinking that Jesus was powerful in and of Himself can stir up doubts about our own ability to follow His example. "I can't do these things because

I am not God," we may reason. But Jesus said in John 12:21, "The works that I do, you will do and even greater works." Jesus did all His mighty works as a man.

Jesus was all God and all man, yet Philippians 2:5-8 tells us He emptied Himself of all His divine attributes: omniscience, omnipotence and omnipresence. Jesus, the all-powerful, all-knowing, eternal and present God, laid all those attributes down and came as a vulnerable baby born in a stable. He did this to identify with you and me.

Jesus made no secret about how He was able to work miracles, but explained it this way for us:

John 5:19 Then Jesus answered and said to them, "Most assuredly, I say to you, the Son can do nothing of Himself, but what He sees the Father do; for whatever He does, the Son also does in like manner."

Spiritual eyesight equips us to do the works of Jesus. Jesus did what He saw His Father doing and many miracles and healings were performed. When we start taking time to look and listen when faced with a need, we also will see the works that Jesus wants performed through us.

Let's look closely at John 5:19 again. In the first part, Jesus says this: "The Son can do nothing of himself." That is an interesting comment. If you assumed that Jesus' capability to heal, do miracles and walk on water was because He is God, you are mistaken. He is God, but that is not how He did the things He did. Jesus identified Himself as the Son of Man. He came to identify with you.

Jesus was God come to earth, but limiting Himself to the condition of a man. He came as the pattern Son so that as we catch His lead, we can follow Him into doing His works. He came as the one who was laying out the footsteps that you and I have to follow. Peter wrote that Jesus came leaving this example that we should follow in His footsteps. If Jesus did His works through His divinity, then we couldn't follow because you can't walk in footsteps that big. But if Jesus walked as the Son of Man on the earth and did the works of His Father through His humanity, then you can follow in His steps.

If you study Philippians 2:6, you read that Jesus did not consider equality with God as something to grab onto, but emptied Himself. He emptied Himself of the attributes of God and came in condition as a man. He left behind those attributes of divinity and Godhead, omniscience and omnipresence.

Omnipresence is one of the attributes of divinity of the Godhead. God is everywhere. Before He descended to earth in human form, He existed in all places everywhere. After He ascended back to heaven again, He re-assumed those attributes. That is why you and I can pray to Him. Wherever two or three meet across the world, He is there, because again He is now omnipresent. But during the period of His ministry on earth He emptied Himself of those attributes of God and was no longer omnipresent. He was here on earth as a baby.

As a human, He was no longer omniscient. He didn't know everything. That's why He asked, "Who touched me?" when the woman with the issue of blood touched Him and received healing. He felt healing virtue flow from Him, but needed to ask who touched Him.

He laid down omnipotence in order to lay down His life and die on the cross to save us from our sins. He could have called on the Father. He could have been rescued from the cross. But this was why He came. To die on the cross, to pay for the penalty of the sin of mankind, to take the authority back from Satan and give it back to us.

Later Jesus arose from the dead, ascended to heaven and resumed all the attributes of omniscience, omnipresence and omnipotence. He is now omniscient again. He is in the position now that He had with the Father before coming to earth. He that descended has ascended and is now Lord of all. That is what scripture tells us.

But when Jesus came to earth, He was born in the same condition as you and me. He willingly chose to empty Himself and come in human condition to suffer all the things that you and I suffer. To experience every limitation, every passion and every area that we suffer, yet without sin. Jesus emptied Himself, came in the condition of a man and then moved in miracles through the work of the Holy Spirit. That is why He could say in John 5:19, "The Son can do nothing of himself." Now if you study that phrase alone, it confirms that He did not use His own power. He became human to give us an example of how we can move in miracles. Later Jesus said the same thing about us, "Without me you can do nothing."

So how did Jesus move in miracles? First of all, the Holy Spirit came upon Him when He was baptized in water. From that time on, He began moving in miracles. If you look at the earthly life of Jesus, there were no miracles that occurred in His life of ministry until the Holy Spirit came upon Him. He went down to the river Jordan where He was baptized in water. When He came up out of the water, the Holy Spirit came upon Him and remained on Him. After that, He was led by the Spirit into the wilderness where He was tested for forty days. From there He went to the wedding feast at Cana where He turned water into wine. The Bible says this was the first of His miracles. There were no miracles before then. It was after the Holy Spirit came upon Him.

Secondly, Jesus looked into heaven and watched to see what the Father was doing and then copied it on earth. This was easy for Him because He spent a lot of time with the Father. He would often spend the whole night in prayer on a mountain or arose early to spend time with Him away from all the crowds. He was intimate with His Father, embracing His love and extending it to the earth. He saw into heaven and did on earth what He saw His Daddy doing. He repeated it faithfully and accurately on earth and miracles happened.

This a beautiful picture of the Father, Son and Holy Spirit working together to impact the affairs of mankind with the power of heaven. This is how the triune God wants to work through you. Miracles occur through an ongoing relationship with Him, not through learning some formula.

If you read in the New Testament all the ways that Jesus healed blind people, you will see that He did not do it by any formula. He made mud with spit and dirt, put it in a blind man's eyes and told him to wash. He returned totally healed. Another time, He simply said, "Your faith has made you whole." Another time He cast out a spirit and a blind and dumb man was healed. Why did He do it differently every time? Because He was watching His Father and doing what He saw from heaven to do.

The divine link that Jesus had to heaven was the Holy Spirit coming upon Him. You and I can have the same experience where the Holy Spirit comes upon us and the Holy Spirit enables us to see what God is doing in heaven. Through the Holy Spirit we are able to see the things that are about to come. That is what it says in John 14, 15 and 16. Many verses in those three chapters tell us what the work of the Holy

Spirit is. He speaks to us, reveals things to us, leads us and guides us. So the Holy Spirit fills us and then we are given the ability to hear from the Lord. We are given the ability to see what the Lord is doing. We are given the ability to catch the initiatives of heaven.

When Jesus left earth and returned to heaven, He commissioned us to do His works. He left us an example of how to do His works when He said, "I only do what I see the Father do." We must do His works, His way. We must catch the initiatives of heaven and do on earth what He is doing in heaven through the Holy Spirit within us. We must activate our spiritual senses that were birthed in us when we gave our lives to Jesus Christ.

A prophetic army of God is arising in these last days to hear from heaven and bring answers to earth. To be the ladder to heaven—by the Holy Spirit. To demonstrate the power of heaven on earth. To bring the abundance of heaven without earthly limitations. To be God's voice to the world and God's loving arms to the lost. To demonstrate the wisdom from above in all sectors of life. That's our commission while we are in our physical bodies.

IT'S TIME TO LIVE FROM ABOVE—
WHERE WE LIVE!

IT'S TIME TO MANIFEST
GOD ON EARTH—
WHERE WE LIVE!

WE DO THIS BY:

Catching
THE INITIATIVES
OF HEAVEN.

Information About Dunamis

Dunamis ARC (Apostolic Resource Center)

In 2004, the Lord began to give us a vision for an Apostolic Resource Center. This would include a school of ministry, a free resource center and a prayer center. The training center would activate people into prophetic evangelism, healing the sick, ministering inner healing and deliverance and would include a biblical foundation. The idea is to bless the whole city and it is open for anyone from around the world wanting to be trained to do the works of Jesus.

We are aware that the Lord is in the process of bringing transformation to His body; that the old styles of ecclesiastic structure will not be sufficient for the tasks at hand. We believe that we are modeling, to some degree, the Christian community of the near future. We also believe that this model and its adaptations will spread around the globe.

Dunamis TI (Training Institute)

Dunamis TI was birthed out of an intense desire to provide in-depth training for people who desire to do the works of Jesus in every place they live. It consists of a short-term, medium-term or long-term training school. The classes include Bible teachings, hands-on practice and street practice. Dunamis Training Institute is open for internship from other nations as well.

Dunamis Power Training

The yearly *Dunamis Power Training* conferences offer three days of intensive teaching and training.

- ► Learn to activate your spiritual senses.
- ► Learn how to move prophetically.
- ► Learn how to move in healing.
- ► Learn how to see and step into heaven.
- ► Learn how to access help from heaven for every need.

For more information, visit **www.DunamisARC.org**.

POPULAR TEACHINGS BY DENNIS WALKER

SINGLE CDs/DVDs

How to Soak in the Spirit—Get started on your adventure with heaven. Learn to get quiet and activate your spiritual senses, so you can experience heaven. With special spontaneous worship at the end by Kelly (Walker) Kallas.

The Spiritual Senses—Just as you have five natural senses to interface with the natural world, so you have five spiritual senses to interface with heaven. Get activated!

The Flow—Learn how to activate spontaneous flow of the Spirit from you to others.

Nine Deadly Embraces—Embracing an offense will take you down a pathway of nine levels of bondage. This teaching will set you free and show you how to free others.

The Secret Place—As you spend intimate times with the Lord, provision for every need on earth is accessed from heaven.

The Garden—Each of us has a garden in heaven to tend like the garden of Eden. This teaching will change your life, your character and your influence on earth.

The Three Heavens—God has a plan for you to possess and live from all three heavens. This will change your life and the world around you.

The Elijah Anointing—God will have a prophetic company in the last days to prepare the way of the Lord.

DVD Sets

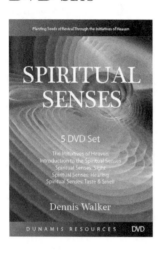

Spiritual Senses
- ► The Initiatives of Heaven
- ► Introduction to the Spiritual Senses
- ► Spiritual Senses: Sight
- ► Spiritual Senses: Hearing
- ► Spiritual Senses: Taste & Smell

Spiritual Life
- ► Living in the Secret Place
- ► The River of Life
- ► The Nine Deadly Embraces
- ► The Heavenly Walk
- ► God's Economy of Needs

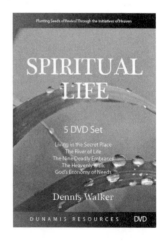

CD Sets

Spiritual Senses
► The Initiatives of Heaven
► Introduction to the Spiritual Senses
► Spiritual Sight
► Spiritual Hearing
► Spiritual Taste & Smell
► Activating the Spiritual Senses

Spiritual Power
► The Initiatives of Heaven
► The Real Heaven
► Open Heaven
► The River of Life
► The Secret Place
► Power Evangelism

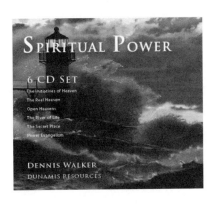

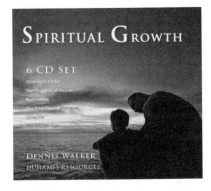

Spiritual Growth
►Abiding in Christ
►The Kingdom of Heaven
►Brokenness
►The Nine Deadly Embraces
►Grow Up!
►The Chosen Fast

Spiritual Intimacy
(by Dennis & Lynnie Walker)

►Ten Ways God Speaks

►Intimacy in Prayer

►How to Soak in the Spirit

►12 Ways to be Led by the Spirit

►Intimacy with God Includes Joy

►Released to Rise Up

These and other teachings from Dennis and Lynnie Walker are available to download for FREE or to purchase CDs or DVDs online from **www.DunamisARC.org**.

OTHER BOOKS PUBLISHED BY DUNAMIS

available at

www.DunamisARC.org

Heavenly Encounters
-a short bio of Lynnie & Dennis Walker

by
Lynnie Walker

In the jungles of Peru, South America, Lynnie and her husband, Dennis Walker, served as young missionaries. In 1985, they moved to Las Vegas, Nevada, in the United States. Wherever they lived, they learned to listen to God and access the power of heaven to do the works of Jesus.

These stories are meant to encourage everyone to believe that heavenly encounters are available, even now, for all who love God, seek Him and do on earth what He's doing in heaven. As people activate their spiritual senses, they can bring the love and power of heaven to earth, causing transformation wherever they go.

Available in English, Spanish, French and German!

TEN WAYS GOD SPEAKS
BY
LYNNIE WALKER

God is speaking all the time. Many say they do not hear Him, but in this book you will find ten of the many ways God speaks. You may be surprised to find that you have been hearing Him all along. It will open you up to an exciting walk with Him.

It is becoming more important to hear God's voice in these last days. In this book, you will receive tips on how to position yourself to hear Him. This will bring blessing into every area of your life as you learn to connect the power of heaven on earth.